Face to Face

"In our increasingly digital world, Brian Grazer takes us on his personal journey of human connection. He proves that the simple step of making eye contact transformed his life and can change yours too. This is a must-read for our time."

> —Neil Blumenthal, co-founder and co-CEO of Warby Parker

"In this digital age, connecting is what humanity is all about. Brian Grazer's captivating and very personal stories are a call to action for us all to see one another. *Face to Face*'s message is essential for our time."

> —Anne Wojcicki, co-founder and CEO of 23andMe

"I remember countless times when Brian made the impossible possible through a single face-to-face conversation. In his new book, he has done a deep dive into the subject of influential face-to-face communication and why it gets things done in business and in life."

> —Ron Howard, Academy Award–winning director

"At a time when human connection is increasingly interrupted by our growing addiction to screens, this captivating book reveals how we can all transform our lives by truly connecting with others. Using highly personal stories, Brian Grazer shows how the simple act of looking up can change your life."

—Arianna Huffington, founder of *Huffington Post*, and CEO of Thrive Global

"Brian's gift is being able to get to the essence of what, and more important, *why* a person feels the way they do. His stories and insights will open your heart and mind to the urgency of human connection."

—Jimmy Iovine, entrepreneur

"I don't know anyone as interesting—or interested—as Brian Grazer. *Face to Face* is a how-to guide to connecting to other people. Nobody else I know could have written it."

—Angela Duckworth, author of *Grit*

"Being connected is not the same thing as connecting. Only when we meet people, face to face, can we form the kinds of meaningful connections that truly matter in our lives. And Brian Grazer is the master. Told through the stories of his own journey, *Face to Face* is a great reminder and a valuable guide for how we too can connect with people in deeper, more meaningful ways."

—Simon Sinek, optimist and author of *Start With Why* and *Leaders Eat Last*

ALSO BY BRIAN GRAZER

A Curious Mind: The Secret to a Bigger Life

Face to Face

The Art of Human Connection

———————→ ←———————

Brian Grazer

Simon & Schuster

NEW YORK LONDON TORONTO
SYDNEY NEW DELHI

Simon & Schuster
1230 Avenue of the Americas
New York, NY 10020

First Simon & Schuster hardcover edition September 2019

SIMON & SCHUSTER and colophon are registered trademarks
of Simon & Schuster, Inc.

For information about special discounts for bulk purchases,
please contact Simon & Schuster Special Sales at 1-866-506-1949
or business@simonandschuster.com.

The Simon & Schuster Speakers Bureau can bring authors to your
live event. For more information or to book an event, contact the
Simon & Schuster Speakers Bureau at 1-866-248-3049
or visit our website at www.simonspeakers.com.

Interior design by Paul Dippolito

Manufactured in the United States of America

1   3   5   7   9   10   8   6   4   2

Library of Congress Cataloging-in-Publication Data is available.

ISBN 978-1-5011-4772-2
ISBN 978-1-5011-4774-6 (ebook)

For my wife, Veronica,
my soul mate in every way.
You see all of me.

Contents

Introduction

"Brian, look at me when I'm speaking to you!"

It's been a while since I was in elementary school, but I can still remember when my teacher, Miss Jenkins, would call on me. My entire body would break out in a cold sweat. My heart would pound. And my eyes would look anywhere *except* in Miss Jenkins's direction.

Miss Jenkins probably didn't look threatening to anyone else. But she absolutely terrified me. Once, when she thought I wasn't paying attention in class, she took me outside the room and hit me across the face with a wooden paddle, leaving a throbbing, red welt across my cheek. More than Miss Jenkins's temper, though, what truly petrified me was her ability to make me feel humiliated just by asking me a question. I almost *never* knew the answer, and being forced to admit that—time after time, out loud, in front of the whole class—was mortifying. The other students snickered behind my back and whispered jokes at my expense. It hurt worse than a paddle to the face. I dreaded going to school every morning because I anticipated another question from Miss Jenkins, and more humiliation.

Needless to say, short of hiding under my desk (tempting though it was), I did everything I could to stay off Miss Jenkins's radar. When she asked a question, scanning the room for a response, I would turn my head or fake a cough. I came up with all kinds of excuses: bathroom breaks, stomachaches, even a feigned broken toe. But my avoidance technique of choice was "the Look-Away." At this age, hiding my eyes was the ultimate way to disconnect. I figured, if I didn't meet Miss Jenkins's eyes, she wouldn't call on me. Disaster averted. When I saw other students using the same move, I understood that they were probably averting their eyes to avoid embarrassment too.

Of course, my attempts to evade my teacher's attention weren't always successful. On those days when she called my name, rather than glance in her direction to signal I'd heard, I'd continue to stare at the ceiling . . . or the chalkboard . . . or my feet. If I didn't look at her, I thought, maybe she would look away too. Maybe she would take pity on me and move on to someone else. Maybe I would disappear entirely and she wouldn't see me anymore. It was a far-flung hope. But it was worth a shot if it meant that I could avoid looking clueless, yet again, in front of my friends and classmates.

The truth is, school was hard for me. The reason I had trouble answering questions in class was that I had trouble doing my homework; and the reason I had trouble doing my homework was because reading was incredibly difficult for me. I'd look at the words, but they made no sense. I couldn't sound them out. I couldn't connect the symbols on the page with the language I knew and used every day. In retrospect, I understand that I was dealing with a reading disability. Unfortunately, this was way back before it might have been more readily identified as "dyslexia." At the time, people just assumed that if your reading skills were weak it was because you were lazy or stupid.

I don't think my situation at home made things any easier. More often than not, I'd barely survive a day at school just to come home to find my parents arguing. They were constantly bickering—at times full-out yelling at each other—and a lot of their fights seemed to be about what to do with me and whether to hold me back a grade. But they rarely talked to me about it. Long story short, as a kid, I felt alone and anxious, pretty much all the time.

It was really thanks to my beloved grandma, Sonia, that I was able to gain some confidence and change my relationship with academics as I entered high school. A classic, four-foot-ten Jewish grandmother, she always believed in me and tried to reinforce my areas of strength, one of which was verbal communication. See, I've always been a better talker than reader. Grandma Sonia would grab my hand and tell me, "Brian, you've got the gift of gab. You're going all the way!" and "Never stop asking those questions of yours!" The more I embraced these messages internally, the more assured I became at school. I started to ask questions and contribute to discussions voluntarily. Rather than avoid my teachers, I engaged and connected with them. It wasn't long before I realized that when I looked at my teachers and classmates while they were speaking, I was better able to absorb what they were saying. The more focused I was, the more intently I listened, the easier it was to understand the material. It turns out that all that time I had been trying to disengage in elementary school, hiding my eyes so that the teacher wouldn't call on me, I was making learning even harder for myself.

Once I got to the University of Southern California, the stakes were raised and the pressure to do well intensified. College was an entirely different playing field, and I had to be even more resourceful to master what I wanted—and needed—to learn in order to do well out in the world after I graduated. Building on the habits I started to develop as a teenager, I became laser-focused on my professors and found ways to connect with them beyond the traditional confines of the lectures. I would corner them after class and plant myself at their office hours (my favorite) so we could discuss the material they were teaching. Being able to ask questions in an intimate environment where we could look each other face to face brought the subject matter to life for me in new ways.

Study groups had similar benefits. In face to face gatherings with my peers, I learned both from what was being said and what wasn't. People became my human guidebooks and cheat sheets. I grew adept at listening to them and reading their nonverbal cues, from their expressions to their body language. I noticed that when I focused on someone, they could feel I was interested in them and were more apt to keep talking and sharing with me. During these conversations, I asked questions that made what we were learning in class more personally relevant, things like: "Why do we care about this lecture on physics? How does it apply to real life?" Or I asked probing questions about their thoughts and feelings, things like: "Why did you do that?" and "How did that affect you?" Sometimes we would spar, sometimes agree, but the back-and-forth exchanges were far more interesting than the one-way communication method of a lecture. Through these, I absorbed as much information as I could, nurturing my intellect and starting to expand my world. Not to mention that I enjoyed them immensely!

In my junior year, I decided to take an Advanced Chemistry class with some of the smartest kids in the school. After the first class, I realized that I might be in over my head. However, as the semester went on, I noticed that I was asking more insightful, more thoughtful questions than most of my classmates were. I could see the respect in my professor's eyes when I asked him what he thought were the most unsolved mysteries in chemistry, and I remember the exact moment when it occurred to me, *Maybe I'm one of the smart kids.* Amazingly, the more I connected with others, the more I got out of my education and the more confident

I became. It was like I had a superpower that was just starting to emerge.

Once I recognized this skill, my life legitimately started to change for the better. I know it sounds trite but it's true. And that pretty much explains how I got here. I never imagined myself writing books. I've always made movies and television. But after years of indulging my curiosity and conducting what I call "curiosity conversations"—conversations with interesting strangers that I use to learn about someone or something new—I decided to write my first book, *A Curious Mind: The Secret to a Bigger Life*. In it, I explore the joys of curiosity and its power to transform our lives. Then, I started to think about how these curiosity conversations have really worked—what made them so impactful. I quickly realized that it was the ability to connect with someone—to look them in the eye and signal to them that I wanted to actually listen to them and learn from them. Figuring out how to connect has probably been the most important skill I've learned in life, and I use it every day: in negotiations, on movie sets, with friends, and especially in new situations. Human connection is my antidote to living a life that would have been more defined by my learning disability. Instead, I found these skills and they've made my life so full.

What I know about connection comes from my own experience and instincts. There is compelling research, however, to back up my personal truth. Harvard researcher, Dr. Robert Waldinger, for instance, has found that "people who are more socially connected to family, friends, and community are happier, healthier, and live longer than people who are less well connected." Other studies show that good relationships appear to protect our brains, helping our memories stay sharper longer. This suggests that staying connected should be just as important as exercise or a good diet when it comes to taking care of ourselves.[1]

When I read these kinds of studies and think about the profound impact the ability to connect has had on me, I can't help but worry. In today's world, we seem to be losing this key ingredient to our health, happiness, and success. Everything is always go, go, go. We don't take the time to really see the people in front of us; we are not patient enough to stick with the gradual process of building meaningful relationships. Instead, the modern impulse is for quick, transactional communication. I find this to be especially true in business, where people can be more interested in "getting ahead" and "getting it done" than getting to know one another—what motivates someone else, what they care about. When actually, getting to know one another is almost always the most effective path to getting anything done, both in the near term and the long run.

Technology only exacerbates the problem. Think of how often you've seen a couple out at dinner scrolling through their Instagram feeds, both engrossed in their phones instead of each other. Or parents tapping away at their screens while their kids vie for their attention. Or a room full of executives looking at their email instead of paying attention to the person presenting. Every day we seem to take another step away from the vital practice of interacting with the people right in front of us. Now, I'm the first to acknowledge the benefits of having a mobile computer in our hands, and yes, I am known to post breakfast videos from my backyard. But the more preoccupied we become with devices and the more social media monopolizes our attention, the more we seem to be sacrificing real connections for virtual ones, and the rewards of these mediated relationships just aren't the same.

Despite the fact that we're more "connected" than ever before, isolation and loneliness are increasingly serious issues for many of us. In one study of Americans ages 19 to 32, the top 25 percent of social media users were *twice* as likely to report feeling lonely as the people using it least. Sure, loneliness existed long before the internet and social media, but we seem to have reached a new level of alienation. Nearly half of all Americans today say they are lonely[2] and in the UK the problem was severe enough to warrant the appointment of the first "Minister for Loneliness."[3] I would venture to say that people today are starving for genuine relationships, a sense of belonging, and the feeling of being known and understood.

A major reason we are becoming so bad at forming connections is because we are losing the ability, the opportunity, and the desire to look others in the eye. The more we attend to our devices rather than the people in front of us and the more we send messages via text, email, and social media rather than meeting and talking face to face, the more comfortable we become looking down at our screens rather than up at one another. And the loss is huge. Research now tells us that babies who don't have sufficient eye contact are at more risk for neural and brain disorders, and that children and adults who are denied eye contact tend to have more psychological problems.[4] But I don't need these studies to tell me what I already know. All I have to do is think about how much I missed out on in elementary school, when I spent all my time trying *not* to look at my teacher.

We, of course, use many tools during face to face contact that help us communicate more clearly and navigate relationships. For me, however, eye contact is far and away the most critical. It's like the wifi of human connection. Just as wifi connects us to endless information on the internet, making eye contact opens up endless possibility. One look is enough to capture someone's attention, spark engagement, ignite attraction, and create a bridge to real connection. In addition to making me a more focused, active listener, being able to look someone in the eye puts me in a mindful state and makes me more self-aware. It gives me internal power and confidence. And that draws people in.

No one wants to open up with someone who is looking at everyone and everything else in the room. No one wants to keep sharing with someone fixated on their phone. Looking someone in the eyes with genuine interest signals to them that you are present with and for them. And that is the start-ing point for respect and validation. It signals that they mat-ter. It is the jumping off point for everything that is essential in a meaningful relationship—curiosity, trust, intimacy, em-pathy, and vulnerability. When we look someone in the eyes, really look at them, we are telling them *I see you.* We are rec-ognizing their humanity. And they, in turn, have the chance to recognize ours.

Although this might sound like it's only relevant to per-sonal relationships, I can tell you firsthand that it makes a huge difference in *all* kinds of relationships. In fact, your ability to make eye contact can be the determining factor in whether or not you get a job, earn the trust of your cowork-ers, or get the greenlight on a project you're pitching. It can make or break your career. Yes, a thing as small as looking someone in the eye is that powerful. After all, whether or not we're at the office or in some other professional context, we're still human.

In a world where our attention is too often focused down-ward or elsewhere, simply lifting your eyes to meet anoth-er's gaze can be transformative. Today, whether in business or socially, I am surprised and struck when someone makes really good eye contact. When a person looks calmly into my soul, and is genuinely interested in my existence, it feels unique and real. And I remember them for it. In our chaotic world of perpetual busyness and distraction, eye contact just might be the ultimate differentiator.

Try this quick experiment and you'll start to understand what I mean. For one day, put your phone away—out of sight—in every meeting, at every meal, and during any conversation. Look each person you interact with in the eye. As you hold eye contact with them, focus on what they are saying. Be present and listen. Notice how your interactions change. Be aware of how it makes you feel. And watch as it makes others feel more respected, heard, seen, and valued. Chances are, they will reciprocate.

One of the best things about eye contact is that it's completely democratic. The ability to look someone in the eye doesn't require money or special equipment or membership in any elite club. It's not about who you know or what you do. With a little intention, courage, and practice, anyone can do it. That doesn't mean it's easy. It wasn't until I was well into my twenties that I was able to (almost) regularly look people in the eye and feel comfortable and calm. I'm so glad I pushed through the awkwardness to get there, though, because it has made all the difference. This simplest of behaviors—the one step of looking another person in the eye—has changed everything about how I show up in the world, how I get filled up, and how I give back.

As humans, all of us seek deep, soulful, genuine connection with other humans. It's what it means to be alive. I view every interaction in my life, even and especially the smallest— whether it be with the person standing next to me in line for coffee or disentangling their dog from mine at the park—as an invitation to connect. This is a book full of stories about how those connections have transformed my life. Without exception, all of the stories I write about have one thing in common: No matter where I was or who I was with, every connection was made possible by a face to face interaction and a look in the eye. Choosing to see another person is a simple, split-second decision we make multiple times, every day. I hope that reading about my personal experiences will inspire you to prioritize face to face encounters in your own life and encourage you to start looking up and truly *seeing* each other. Make the choice, and watch how your life starts to transform in the most profound ways.

CHAPTER 1

Do You See Me?

*"What we're all striving for is authenticity,
a spirit-to-spirit connection."*

—Oprah

In my early twenties, I fell into an entry-level law clerk position at Warner Brothers. The majority of my job consisted of delivering documents to important people around town. In other words, it was drudge work. However, I had an active mind and a penchant for creativity, and it wasn't long before I figured out how to turn my boring job into an exciting opportunity. I had already figured out in school that I learned best when I connected with people. So, I thought, why not try that approach in "real life" and use it to help me figure out my career?

I was in the world of Hollywood now. *How did this world work? Would I stay there? What would I do? How would I forge a path?* I had tons of questions. Finding the answers turned out to be easier than you might suspect. As a law clerk, I spent my days bouncing between the offices of famous and powerful industry players. All I had to do was tell their assistants that the urgent papers I was delivering would be invalid unless I handed them directly to the boss. Just like that, I was in. Soon enough, I was having conversations with writers, directors, producers, studio heads, agents, you name it—anyone who could help me better understand the mysteries of the movie business.

I set this goal for myself: I had to meet one new person in the industry every single day. It worked so well, and I learned so much, that I decided to extend my reach. I added a second goal: to meet at least one person every two weeks *outside* of Hollywood. Again, the experiences were better than I could have imagined. It wasn't just that I was gaining information, I was engaging in meaningful exchanges that left me feeling inspired, uplifted, and curious to know even more.

Although I eventually gave up my specific goals for meeting people, I have never stopped having what I now call "curiosity conversations." For the past forty years, I have been tracking down people about whom I am curious and asking if I can sit down with them for an hour. Sometimes this results in meetings with several new people a week. I have no other motive than to learn something from them that will broaden my mind and alter my understanding of the world. It's also important to me that my conversation partner benefit as well, so I try to ask thought-provoking questions that might ignite insights for them as well. In addition, I am sure to bring some kind of gift or some knowledge they would find useful or interesting. When I met with George W. Bush, I gave him a baseball cap with the logo from my show *Fri-*

day Night Lights, which was set in Texas. When I met with Dr. Dre, I came ready to tell him about the theme song to *Exodus*, thinking he would enjoy it because his own music contains beautiful and spectactular melodies.

Today, as a movie and television producer, I look for people who are experts in anything *other* than what I do, hoping to find what moves and inspires them. I love getting to know the heartbeat of people from all types of backgrounds— from spies and Nobel laureates to athletes and tech entrepreneurs. I've been honored to meet with artistic giants like Andy Warhol, Catherine Opie, Jeff Koons, and Mark Bradford (who generously created the *Face to Face* artwork for this book), as well as heads of state including Barack Obama, Ronald Reagan, Margaret Thatcher, King Abdullah II lbn Al Hussein of Jordan, Mohammad bin Salman, and Benjamin Netanyahu. I've picked the brain of iconic investor Warren Buffett, Spanx creator Sara Blakely, renowned science fiction writer Isaac Asimov, and so many others. A few years ago, I captured the best of these conversations in my book, *A Curious Mind*. Since then, I've enjoyed countless other conversations with interesting and accomplished strangers, some of whom I now call friends. I'll quickly share a few of these here.

Not too long ago, I sat in my living room with rapper-activist Sonita Alizadeh. At seventeen, Sonita wrote and recorded a rap song protesting forced marriage after learning her family intended to sell her off as a child bride for nine thousand dollars. The song went viral, and she became a hero to the many girls facing this oppressive life sentence. With lyrics like "I scream to make up for a woman's lifetime of silence," the song became an anthem in her home country of Afghanistan.[5] With long black hair and big, beaming eyes, she exudes a calm confidence considering all she has been through in her life. As a child, Sonita and her family fled Afghanistan to escape the oppressive rule of the Taliban. Instead, she had to scrub bathroom floors to support herself and her family while also managing to teach herself how to read and write. Listening to the radio as she cleaned, she became enamored by the music of Iranian rapper Yas as well as Eminem. In rap music she discovered an outlet for self-expression and began to write her own songs about child labor. Haunted by the memories of her many friends in Afghanistan who had disappeared one by one from the classroom to be sold off as child brides, she could no longer remain silent. Though it is illegal in Iran for women to sing or rap, and incredibly dangerous to speak out, she would hide her lyrics in her backpack. When she heard about a contest in the United States to write a song to get Afghan people to vote, she entered her song and won the one-thousand-dollar prize. She sent the money to her mother, who had moved back to Afghanistan.

Soon after, Sonita wrote a rap song called "Brides for Sale" to give voice to all the children facing forced marriage. She played the video for me, sharing in a soft yet serious voice that she was just ten years old when her own mother first considered selling her to a man.

In the video, Sonita speaks out against this practice dressed in a white wedding dress, her body adorned with painted-on bruises, and a bar code across her forehead. She pleads into the camera not to be sold. The video went viral with over a million views to date, and earned her a full scholarship to a music school in Utah.

With her deep and compassionate eyes, Sonita told me that she does not resent her mother for trying to sell her; she understands that this was how the older generation was raised. Instead of hanging on to the past, Sonita is looking forward, trying to change tradition and shift culture through community education. Although there is a lot of suffering in the world, she says, there is also a great deal of hope when you put your voice to work for the change you want to see. Sonita's composure and emotional intelligence really struck me. She was still in high school yet spoke with the wisdom of someone far beyond her years. As I sat next to her on the couch listening to her story, I sensed a deep knowing in her.

After we finished our conversation, we made our way to the dining room to have a meal. She was staying at our home that evening, and Veronica and I thought it would be nice to spend time getting to know her as a family. After dessert, Sonita sprung up from the table to go throw a football around the yard with my son Patrick, just like any other teenager. Our time together opened my eyes to a long-standing tradition that subjects millions of girls to a devastating life of violence and servitude. I walked into that conversation having no idea about the life experience of a girl in Afghanistan or Iran, and she gave me a bird's-eye view not only into the factual elements of what life is like—being expected to submit to a lifetime of rape and forced labor—but most important, what it feels like to live in fear and have the courage to rise from oppression. She gave me a whole new understanding of human grace, resilience, and, most of all, hope.

Another memorable conversation I had was with award-winning journalist and "flow" expert Steven Kotler. It was inspired by my experiences of flow state over the years.

I was just starting to film my surf movie *Blue Crush* on the North Shore of Hawaii. Absorbing the surf culture up close, through the eyes of the locals, I found the sport to be irresistible. It was exhilarating to watch and mind-blowing to imagine that the incredibly intense waves of the North Shore are completely created by nature. I would watch surfers eagerly and fearlessly race into twenty- to fifty-foot waves, and come back exhilarated. I wanted to experience it but had never tried to surf before. So it was then, at age forty, that I decided to learn. I befriended a local named Brock who had surfed the biggest paddle-out wave in the world. He was stoic and cool without pretention, and known to be fearless in surfing, fighting, dirt biking, and anything he took on. We immediately had chemistry. He was a natural at teaching—he knew everything about surfing and water safety—and I'm a natural-born learner. We got to work.

He taught me the very basics of how to stand up on a

board as well as the physics of the ocean so I could pick the perfect wave. As my instructor and friend over the years, Brock saved my life many times when we've been out on the water. I often pushed the limits of my abilities because I felt safe with him.

As I became a better surfer, I started to experience flow state. Flow state in surfing is easier to understand when you think of these big-wave surfers like Brock, Laird Hamilton, Keala Kennelly, and Makua Rothman . . . think about any one of them navigating and waiting to intersect with a forty-foot towering wave with enough power to destroy a building, and then being able to mount their board with millisecond precision that has to all be intuited in a flow state to survive the wave. It's literally impossible to measure all of the variables in that single moment. You have to be in flow state not to die.

When I would catch the right kind of wave, I became completely immersed in the moment as I stood up, super aware but no longer worrying about how to balance the board or where to position my feet. It was like slow-motion euphoria, and like nothing I had ever experienced. That fleeting fifteen seconds was so exhilarating and euphoric that I would fly to Indonesia or Hawaii to experience it as often as I could. I became increasingly curious: *Could I transport the ingredients and format of flow state into other endeavors, like playing tennis or one-on-one curiosity conversations, which feel timeless when they're good?* Since I didn't have the answers, I reached out to Steven.

We met for dinner at Giorgio's, an intimate Italian restaurant in Santa Monica, right off the Pacific Coast Highway. Steven walked in, and I immediately liked him. He gave off a fresh, almost vibrating energy. He sat down and we ordered a bottle of red wine. Conversation came easily. Steven was highly alert, so much so that he barely blinked as we spoke. He defined flow as moments of total absorption, when we are fully energized, focused, and immersed in the process of our activity and achieving optimum performance. In these moments, everything else, including space and time, seems to disappear. He was describing exactly those rare moments I felt when surfing, and more recently on the tennis court.

Steven went on to explain that "the zone" or "flow state" is one of the most desirable states of being on earth. It's also one of the most elusive. Seekers have spent centuries trying to reproduce the experience in a consistent and reliable way, but few have succeeded. One exception is action-and-adventure athletes like surfers, skiiers, and climbers who regularly take on terrifying obstacles from towering cliffs to gravity-defying waves. I was curious: *What do these athletes know that I don't? What is their "inner game"?* Steven told me that during a flow state, the brain produces a cascade of performance-enhancing chemicals, such as epinephrine and dopamine, which tighten focus and lower signal-to-noise ratios.[6]

After we finished our entrees, Steven shared that the reason he started to research flow was because he had been struck with Lyme disease. For three years, the disease had completely disabled him, leaving him bedridden and in pain. The disease was also making him extremely paranoid. He would find himself hallucinating. His short- and long-term memory were gone, and he couldn't read, write, or even recognize the color green. He said it was terrifying, that there's nothing worse than watching yourself go crazy. He was thirty years old and thought about ending his life.

One day, a friend prodded Steven to go surfing in the hope that it would lift his spirits. The activity left him so physically exhausted that he could barely get out of bed for the next two weeks. But as soon as he felt better, Steven did it again. And then again. Each time he surfed, he entered into an altered state of consciousness. He explained that this flow state flushed all the stress hormones out of his system, and pumped his body full of performance enhancers. It reset his nervous system, and ultimately helped cure his Lyme disease.[7] I was riveted.

For weeks following that evening at Giorgio's, I spent my early morning time digesting YouTube videos, articles, interviews, and anything interesting I could find on flow. This led me to think about the overall concept of altered mind states, and I started reading Michael Pollan's book, *How to Change Your Mind*, about the effect of psychedelics on our consciousness. I've never tried drugs, yet I'm curious about what he has to say about how they can positively affect our well-being. It's not unusual for curiosity conversations to take me on these kinds of journeys of exploration, with each meeting whetting my appetite to learn more. (And yes, I'm now reaching out to Pollan to see if he will meet with me for a conversation!)

Every curiosity conversation is different. I always prepare for them as best I can, but what I've found is that the key to a fulfilling interaction depends on much more than showing up with a list of questions. In fact, while it's important to be prepared, it's even more important to show up with the capacity for wonderment and openness, a beginner's mind, really. Approaching these meetings with no end point in mind is what makes them *conversations* rather than rigid, agenda-driven interviews. When you enter into conversation with someone, you *must* pay attention to what they are saying if you want the exchange to go anywhere. And paying attention starts with the eyes.

The basic habit of looking other people in the eye is the starting point for *why* my curiosity conversations work and why they are so exciting. If curiosity is the engine that gets me in the room with another person and propels the conversation, eye contact is the ignition point. It is the first step in truly getting to know someone and creating a real connection.

In a curiosity conversation, looking at someone with calm, centered, interested eyes helps me focus, listen, formulate questions, and move the discussion forward. It also sends a message that is critical to the success of the conversation. It says *I am present.* When you show someone that you are paying attention to them with your eyes, you are also communicating that you sincerely want to get to know them. You are taking the time and energy to focus on them because they matter; their knowledge, thoughts, insights, experiences are of value. There is not one person on earth, regardless of their industry, status, or passions, who doesn't crave that kind of validation, whether they admit it or not. In my experience, when you are able to give people that, they are more likely to talk openly and honestly about who they are and why they do the things they do. And often they will want to know about you, too.

We've all heard the truism that love isn't a one-way street. In fact, no connection, even one made between strangers, is. Think about your own experiences at work or at home. If your daughter comes home and you tell her all about your day without asking anything about hers, the moment is likely to fall flat. The same is true if you are talking to someone who wants to tell you everything about their life but expresses no interest in yours.

A one-way soul grab never works. It has to be mutually fulfilling. The best curiosity conversations are the ones where both people are engaged, contributing, and learning from each other. We're absorbed in each other's eyes, listening, empathizing, and, sometimes, even reaching a place of vulnerability and trust. There is a give and take, which fosters intimacy.[8] When that happens, there is (almost) nothing like it. I often find myself thinking, "Wow, this is like being on the most fantastic date." When I feel the chemistry of a real connection, I don't want it to end.

Although eye contact was always key to my curiosity conversations, I wasn't practicing it consciously or even aware that I was doing it in the beginning. It wasn't something I thought about and certainly wasn't an approach I'd adopted in my everyday encounters. It never even crossed my mind to do so. Until Ron Howard called me out.

After my delivery days with Warner Brothers were over, I went to work for a hot-tempered television VP named Edgar Scherick. Scherick offered me a deal I couldn't refuse: "Whatever you can sell, you can make." So, I sold a TV movie. It did really well and led to other well-received projects, including a prestigious series on the Ten Commandments. I used my success to leverage an exclusive contract with Paramount. That's where I met Ron. Ron, who was an actor, wanted to direct movies, and I wanted to produce them. And so our partnership began. Together, we co-founded Imagine Entertainment, where we've been partners for the last thirty-five years and counting.

Even back in our twenties, Ron always had exceptional communication skills. One day, in his kind way, he shared an observation with me.

"Do you realize you seldom look other people in the eye when we're meeting with them?" Ron asked.

It was 1980, and we were sitting in my office on the same Paramount lot where we met. We had just spent time with the writers Lowell Ganz and Babaloo Mandel, who would later go on to write *Night Shift*, *Splash*, and other movies with us. I had been multitasking, as was my habit during meetings back then. I would read something or jot down a list of what I had to do that week while others were talking. I wasn't thinking about it. It's just what I did.

In 2019, I know that multitasking when people are trying to talk to you isn't good. It's not only disrespectful, but it sucks the air out of the room. At the time, however, I didn't immediately grasp what Ron was trying to tell me.

"What do you mean?" I responded.

"Were you really listening to what Lowell and Babaloo were saying?"

"Of course," I said. "I heard every word of it."

"Maybe," Ron said, "but you weren't *looking* at them. If you don't look at them when they're talking, it hurts their feelings."

"But I heard everything," I said.

"It doesn't matter," he said. "If you don't look people in the eye when they talk, they don't feel respected."

This struck me. I distinctly remembered being on the receiving end of this sort of behavior. At the outset of my career, I'd met one of the most powerful agents in Hollywood. He never looked me in the eye; instead, he looked right through me or right past me whenever I saw him or tried to talk to him. It made me feel like a nobody because I could tell that he didn't care one bit about what I had to say. We've all had that experience, of meeting someone at a party who looks over our shoulder while they talk to us. It never feels good. But it wasn't until Ron pointed it out to me that I realized I might have sometimes been doing this myself! I couldn't help but wonder if my actions were making people feel the way I had felt with that agent.

The influence of that tip-off from Ron can be seen in *Night Shift*, the first movie we made together. The hero of *Night Shift* is Bill Blazejowski, played by Michael Keaton. Bill is a young guy who, after being fired from a series of jobs, comes up with the idea to operate a prostitution ring while working the graveyard shift at the New York City morgue. Although this particular venture wasn't one I'd undertaken, Bill's story was inspired by my early struggles with keeping down a job. Drawing on the advice from Ron, I decided to give Bill an exaggerated trait—a severe inability to maintain eye contact. Every time a new hustle popped into his head, Bill's eyes would bounce around wildly. It was clear that his mind was somewhere else, not focused on whomever he was with in that moment. He was a hustler who didn't yet know that eye contact equals respect. It was an odd characteristic for a character in a comedy. But for me personally, it was a friendly reminder to correct my own behavior.

Ron's feedback also had a direct impact on my interactions with others. From the moment he pointed out my lack of eye contact, I resolved to always look at others during meetings. As soon as I did, something magical began to happen. The meetings no longer felt plainly transactional. I felt more in sync with people than I had in the past. I was able to gain insights that I wouldn't have picked up if I had been looking away, like how much belief they had—or didn't have—in a project. People could tell I was paying attention and they felt respected. As a result, they had more respect for me and more genuine interest in what I had to say. There was a new sense of reciprocity.

If this all sounds familiar, it's because it is. It's the same thing that happens during my curiosity conversations. I naturally go into those conversations eager to learn from and about another person. That eagerness shows in my rapt gaze and the door to connection opens up from there. It hadn't occurred to me to think about all of my face to face encounters this way. Now, of course, it seems like the simplest thing. Everyone wants to feel seen, heard, respected, and valued— not just the people I invite to sit down with me for a curiosity conversation. And the truth is, every person has the potential to teach us something new or show us a new way of looking at the world. All we have to do to unlock that potential is to acknowledge them through our eyes and invite them to connect.

CHAPTER 2

Take a Chance on Connection

*"Staying vulnerable is a risk we have to take
if we want to experience connection."*

—Brené Brown, *The Gifts of Imperfection*

Oprah Winfrey is arguably the most gifted communicator in the world. Her empathetic eyes combined with her perceptible warmth serve to disarm even the most closed off interviewees, who inevitably open up and share their innermost feelings and life stories with her. It's a phenomenon I've experienced firsthand.

As I described in *A Curious Mind*, I first met Oprah at a moment when my life was at something of a low ebb. We had agreed to meet for breakfast at the Hotel Bel-Air, where she was staying. Oprah was with her longtime best friend, Gayle King, a major talent in her own right as a journalist and television anchor. At that time in my life, I was in the midst of a romantic crisis. Normally, it takes me a little time to open up, but somehow I trusted Oprah right away. I felt like I already *knew* her. Suddenly, I found myself pouring my heart out to her, divulging feelings I had never shared with anyone else. There was something about the quality of Oprah's attention, the way she leaned in and held my gaze that made me feel like she saw me and she cared about me. Not only did she play back the things I said, she had a gift for helping me synthesize and clarify my thoughts and feelings. She would say things like, "So, in other words, it sounds as though you must believe *this*, based on how you were feeling about *that*..." Oprah helped me understand *myself* better. Connecting with her was an incredibly powerful experience that has never left me.

Years later, when Oprah invited me on her show *Super-Soul Sunday* to talk about my book, a similar thing happened. I was used to doing press for movies and TV shows I'd produced, but the publicity tour for the book was much more personal. Because the book was about my own life experiences, talking about it made me feel vulnerable and uneasy. Now I was being asked to be the sole focus of an hour-long show about diving deep into your own soul. Driving to Oprah's home in Montecito, where interviews for the show often take place, waves of anxiety washed over me.

When I arrived at my destination, the gate opened, and we pulled up the long driveway. As soon as I saw Oprah, dressed in a bright green shirt, walking across the lawn toward me, my nerves just melted away. I immediately felt comfortable and safe. I could breathe. The feeling didn't come from any words she said. It came from the way her face lit up as our eyes met in greeting. I felt understood.

In her 2013 commencement speech at Harvard University, Oprah explained her observations about human beings this way:

"I have done over thirty-five thousand interviews in my career, and as soon as that camera shuts off, everyone always turns to me and inevitably, in their own way, asks this question: 'Was that okay?' I heard it from President Bush. I heard it from President Obama. I've heard it from heroes and from housewives. I've heard it from victims and perpetrators of crimes. I even heard it from Beyoncé in all her Beyoncéness . . . They all want to know one thing: Was that okay?"[9]

Deep down, all of us have doubts and insecurities. We use people's eyes as a gauge to see whether we can trust them. When we find openness and attentiveness there, we are more likely to let ourselves be vulnerable and share. When we feel listened to, we feel understood and validated. When we feel understood and validated, we like a person. When we like a person, we trust them. And when we trust them, we're more inclined to bare our essential and authentic selves. In order to form deep and meaningful bonds that transcend small talk and cookie-cutter conversation, we have to get to this place.

A big part of the reason people open up when face to face with Oprah is because they can see sincere interest and concern in the way she looks at them. Oprah is unreservedly herself, and she makes others want to be the same in her presence. I have a tremendous admiration for Oprah in this regard, and strive to approach others with honesty and authenticity.

I find that if I'm not pushing myself to be as true and raw as I can be when I am face to face with someone, then I'm not maximizing the moment for them or me. If I'm guarded and just skimming the surface with them, then I might as well not be there. If I'm hiding my authentic self by trying to impress or be something I'm not, then I am denying both of us the chance for a true soul to soul connection.

Meeting another person's gaze can feel awkward, frightening, even embarrassing at times. Being "real" with another person isn't always comfortable either—many times it's not. But I have learned that if we want to form connections in our lives that actually mean something, we have to make ourselves vulnerable.

Before the proliferation of cell phones, when I would arrive early to an event or when I found myself alone with a stranger (in an elevator, say), I felt compelled to speak to them, or at least to acknowledge their presence. I think we all felt this way. But these days, we're more apt to look down at our phones, getting lost in the scroll of our social media feed or our mounting inbox, because we're not sure how to start a conversation, or whether the other person even wants to engage in a conversation with us at all.

It takes a bit of courage to take a chance on a connection. After all, our interest, attention, or gaze may not be reciprocated. And because we, as humans, are all insecure in some way, we often assume that we are the reason why: *Is it the way I look? Maybe I'm not interesting? Or important enough? Or smart enough?* But usually that's not the case.

Sometimes people just aren't in the frame of mind to want to connect. It's not the right time or circumstance. Or maybe we need to work on our technique a little more. Research suggests that the ideal length of time to hold a person's gaze if you want to form an authentic connection is seven to ten seconds (three to five if you are in a group).[10] Any longer than that can turn people off and start to feel creepy. If someone isn't responding to you, you might want to consider whether you crossed the threshold? Did your glance turn into a stare? Did you stand too close? Maybe your energy felt forced. Maybe you came across as wanting something. Next time you're in a similar situation, try to do something differently.

The other possibility, of course, is that your attempt to connect isn't catching because the other person is awkward, shy, or insecure. Maybe they aren't comfortable being vulnerable because of the environment they grew up in or bad experiences in the past. You may never know why they are hesitant to receive your offer of a connection. But I've found that if you can push through the uncomfortableness, there's a good chance that you'll eventually get that spark that you're looking for.

When I first decided to make the film that would eventually become *8 Mile*, I knew only that I wanted to make a movie about hip-hop. I'd gotten to know some of its iconic figures—Slick Rick, Ol' Dirty Bastard, RZA, Chuck D—pretty early on, and by the time the nineties rolled around, I was fully aware that hip-hop sat at the very center of life for young people in America. One night I debated a prominent *New York Times* journalist, who insisted that hip-hop was simply an inferior, niche culture, one among many, that wouldn't last long. This seemed ridiculous to me. If history has taught us anything, it's that what is cool with the kids now will be mainstream tomorrow. It was clear to me that the dominant culture of the youth generation was on a trajectory to become *the* dominant culture. The *Times* journalist thought he was on the inside looking out, when in fact it was the other way around. But he was far from the only one who didn't get it.

Disconnected from what was actually happening in society, most establishment voices at that time couldn't see how important hip-hop was and wouldn't give it the respect it deserved. This frustrated me, and I wanted to change it. So I decided to make a movie that would convey the power of the hip-hop movement. A film in which hip-hop itself would be the protagonist. Instead of starting off with a story, I started with a theme and a strong point of view.

After hearing what I had in mind, Dr. Dre and Jimmy Iovine introduced me to Marshall Mathers (Eminem). I had never met him before, but I was intrigued. He'd had a hit record, but he wasn't a superstar quite yet. I was drawn to what I knew about his underdog background and to his original and groundbreaking music. Eminem's music brought together a unique combination of ingredients: the voice of the inner city; the humor and irony of his alter ego, Slim Shady; and pop culture. I thought it was brilliant.

Eminem came into my office and right away seemed defensive. He greeted me with a steely-eyed, icy glare. There was no warmth at all. He sat down on my couch and did the best he could not to look at me—or connect with me on any level—for the better part of thirty minutes.

Maybe you've encountered versions of this, moments where the person you're with won't emerge, not even briefly, to accept the attention you are offering. Looking back, I recognize that he didn't have anything against me personally. He was a social introvert, which is ironically common with extremely gifted artists.

The minutes dragged on painfully. I tried everything I could to infuse the room with positive energy and make Marshall feel safe enough to let his guard down. I struggled to show him my soul and make clear my intentions. I wanted this movie to portray hip-hop in its most authentic form, and I was deeply interested in Marshall's perspective. But no matter how hard I tried to engage him in conversation, no matter how specific or inviting the questions I asked, he simply wouldn't respond. It was excruciating. Finally, he'd had enough. He heaved up off the couch.

"I'm out."

I could've just let him go. It wouldn't have been the first—

or the last—time a meeting fell flat, with no connection established. But I made a split-second decision. I jumped up and made a last plea.

"Come on." I looked him straight in the eyes and paused. Then, and I'm not sure where this came from other than desperation, I asked, "You can animate?"

My move could easily have backfired, or come off as too aggressive, because he looked at me, at first, like he was angry. To my surprise—and relief—however, he sat back down and started talking. He told me about where he was from and how he got his start as a rapper. The conversation lasted for almost an hour, and the story he shared with me that day essentially became *8 Mile.*

I later found out that the word "animate" derives from the Latin "anima," which means life, soul, or spirit. I could've picked any word that day with Marshall, but somehow, instinctively, I chose the one that said I was looking for his soul. And it was enough to get him to see me too.

There is no one clear path or prescription to connecting with someone. It doesn't always happen right away. Sometimes it requires patience. Other times you just have to try and break down the wall, like I did with Marshall, and see what happens. Sure, you might ruin any chance of forming a connection. But, is that really worse than playing it safe and leaving with no connection made?

Marshall didn't entirely open up to me during that first meeting. But at least he was willing to stay and talk. And that was enough to lay the groundwork to gradually build a deeper connection.

Eminem and I made *8 Mile* together and he ended up winning an Oscar for best original song. In fact, "Lose Yourself" was the first hip-hop song ever to win an Oscar. My love and respect for hip-hop has only deepened over the years, showing up in my work through the series *Empire*, the scripted drama series *Wu-Tang: An American Saga*, the documentary *Made in America* with Jay-Z, and the upcoming biopic on prolific trap artist Gucci Mane. Hip-hop is now the most popular genre in the world, making a profound impact throughout the culture, from sports and technology to media and fashion; finally there is no dispute that hip-hop is *the* dominant culture of our time.

CHAPTER 3

The "Key" to Serendipity

*"The beauty of a woman must be seen from in
her eyes, because that is the doorway to her heart,
the place where love resides."*

—Audrey Hepburn

Seven years ago, I ended a relationship that I had been in for
a few months. I thought I might take a break from dating for a
while. My neighbor Barbara lived a few doors down from me
in Malibu with her husband, Roy. I'd known her for over a decade. She's a confident, beautiful Italian woman who brings
a certain fierceness to everything she puts her mind to. She
had seen me go through my share of bad relationships and
breakups and suggested we go out to dinner to catch up. I
was looking forward to it because Barbara knows me so well;
in fact, we often warmly greet each other with the likes of "Hi,
brother," or "Great to see you, sister!"

Along with Barbara's best friend, Max, who was visiting
from Italy, we headed to Capo, a restaurant in Santa Monica. Capo is a coveted reservation in this beach town. I love
the food there—my favorites are the branzino cooked over
a wood-burning fire and the grilled Caesar salad—and the

place itself is rustic and cozy yet elegant. We were having a good time over dinner, enjoying a great bottle of Barolo. Just as we finished our entrées, I noticed an incredibly attractive woman in a red dress walk in. Her wavy blond hair bounced off her shoulders as she turned her head to look at the room. I couldn't quite make out her ethnicity, just that she had an exotic look about her and a radiant life force. As luck would have it, she started heading toward our table. I couldn't take my eyes off her.

"Hi, Veronica!" Barbara called out. She stood to hug and greet her friend. Veronica's eyes seemed to twinkle as she broke into a bright smile. Then, Barbara introduced me. As a show of good manners, I popped up and shook her hand. Our eyes met for a quick moment and I instantly felt an attraction. An unexpected warmth rushed through me.

"Would you like to have a glass of wine with us?" I asked, hoping for a yes. She blinked and politely declined, saying she didn't want to interrupt our dinner.

"I just came by to get my key. Barbara and I went out last night to celebrate my birthday and I forgot it in her purse."

"We just finished dinner; you're not interrupting at all," I said. "Please, join us!"

She took the empty seat, which happened to be next to mine, and we all started talking. It was a few weeks before Christmas, so we chatted about our vacation plans. I was heading to St. Barts with some friends, and she was heading to Pennsylvania to see her family. The conversation was easy and fun, and when Veronica started laughing at a joke, I noticed her mouth. And the shape of her lips. I was so drawn to her I felt like kissing her. We had only known each other for five minutes, yet everything and everyone else in the room seemed to disappear. I was magnetized. I had never felt this way with anyone.

At the end of the evening, we walked out and stood facing each other at the valet. Her eyes were lit with an inner happiness that I've come to learn is exactly what she is all about. I immediately asked for her number and called her the very next morning. We've been together ever since. (After all these years, by the way, I still don't believe that Veronica was just stopping by to get her key back from Barbara. She'll never admit it, but I would venture to say that serendipity and "planned serendipity" might be very close cousins!)

My friend Whitney Wolfe Herd is the charismatic founder and CEO of Bumble, a social network that allows people to make connections in all areas of their lives, from the romantic to the professional. Today, Veronica and I have a lot of friends who have turned to apps like Bumble in order to break out of their patterns and meet people they wouldn't cross paths with in their usual social circles. "It's pretty incredible," Whitney says, "that a swipe and a few keystrokes could possibly change the course of your entire life by leading to a powerful and inspiring human connection in the real world."

Whitney is right. I have seen long-lasting, real-life connections come out of online meetings. But however great Bumble or any other social network may be, virtual interactions can only get you so far. Swiping left or right is transactional. You can't find trust, authenticity, or intimacy using Google. And exchanging texts and emails doesn't give you a chance to really connect spirit to spirit with someone. If what you want is a meaningful relationship that goes beyond the surface, at some point you have to get to know a person face to face. Only then can you read their eyes, body language, and vibe to get clues about their character, what they're really thinking, and whether there is something special between you. This is especially true when it comes to romance.

Personally, I have found that true love always starts with the eyes. A little bit of eye contact with the right person is like a drug. It ignites all our other senses. This is what happened the first time Veronica and I locked eyes. Even though it was a brief look, it was a look that revealed a mutual curiosity. When we see curiosity in the eyes of another person, it validates us. It feels great to know that they want to know more about us, that they see something worthwhile in us. If the chemistry is there, we want to return that feeling. With our eyes—and our body language—we tell the other person that we see them too, and we also want to know more. The desire to connect encourages vulnerability. We begin to open up to each other, and as we do, we find out whether we can trust the other person. If we can, then we become even more vulnerable. We feel safe to expose what's inside—our deepest fears and secret dreams. It's a cycle that begins with eye contact and leads to the most fulfilling of connections, the kind in which you come to know another person completely and you, in turn, are known.

To this day, Veronica and I can have a whole conversation across the room from each other at a party. She can tell just from my eyes when I find something funny and I can tell when she is put off by something. Just the other night we were at a dinner party—the kind where they split up the couples to shake up the conversation. I looked over at Veronica and she widened her eyes in a certain way that she does. One of the guests was telling a very long-winded story about his political views. I had to catch myself from laughing out loud because I knew exactly what she was thinking. I could see that she was ready to jump ship and head home. Using our eyes, we share the inside joke or the story in our head. We get exactly what the other is thinking and always have a lot of laughs about it on our way home.

After all this time, I still can't take my eyes off her.

CHAPTER 4

Together We Rise

"No matter how brilliant your mind or strategy,
if you're playing a solo game, you'll always
lose out to a team."

—Reid Hoffman

I have long been a fan of Spike Lee's films. My appreciation of his work started with *Do the Right Thing*. I was blown away by the film's invention, politically progressive substance, and visual style, with its striking and original color palette. Right away, I wanted to work with him. But another seventeen years would pass before we partnered on a movie.

Spike and I first met in 1990 at the Oscar Nominees Luncheon, where Spike was being honored. It was relatively early in both of our careers. Though young filmmakers, we had both been nominated for Oscars in screenwriting—me for *Splash* in 1984 and him for *Do the Right Thing* then. I told him how much I admired his work and how stunned I was by *Do the Right Thing* in particular. The respect was mutual, and we expressed interest in working together. At the time, however, we couldn't find a subject that aligned for us. Spike was looking for an origin of hip-hop movie; I didn't have the right story for it. And so, the years passed.

In the decade after meeting Spike, I noticed that his projects in Hollywood occasionally ended in some friction. This isn't completely uncommon for gifted filmmakers with strong creative visions. Great artists are nonconformists by nature and tend to resist the homogenizing forces that are rampant in the movie business. Clashes ensue. I don't like things to end badly. That's why early on in my career, I developed a rule. There were always four or five different teams of people on a movie (directors, stars, producers, and writers would lead their respective groups). If I concluded by fact or intuition that things might end poorly for one of those leaders, it would temper my enthusiasm to work with them. So, I considered what I'd observed about Spike seriously.

Eventually, I took on some projects that he seemed interested in pursuing. One of these was *American Gangster*. Spike came in for a meeting. Sitting on the couch in my office, Spike explained his vision for *American Gangster* with exceptional clarity. His ideas were thoughtful and precise, as I'd expected they would be. However, his version didn't align with the way I had envisioned the movie.

"Let's keep trying to find something to do together," I said. I walked him out, trading the usual platitudes.

Just as the elevator arrived, Spike reached back behind him and pulled out a script. To this day, I have no idea where it came from.

"Brian," he said, "*this* is something else. This is something I'd like to do with you."

The script was *Inside Man*, which Imagine owned.

Before I could respond—just before the elevator doors closed between us—Spike reached out and grabbed my hand. For the first time that day, he looked me directly in the eyes. Anyone who knows Spike, or has ever shared eye contact with him, knows the unique character of his gaze—it is patient, deeply sincere, transparent. "I promise you," he said, "this relationship will have a good beginning and a great ending, and that this will be a fantastic experience for you." Now, how he knew to say that—I'd certainly never *told* Spike what my hesitations were—I'll never be quite sure.

Up to that moment, I'd simply meant to say good-bye. But one of my life axioms is to be open to spontaneity, so I embraced the possibility of *this* moment.

Technically speaking, *Inside Man* wasn't even available. We had already hired a director on the project. And yet, whatever I might have thought was impossible to do a second ago, was instantly negated. I couldn't say yes fast enough. I hired him right on the spot.

Spike did direct *Inside Man*, and the project was one of the most positive experiences in my career, not to mention a box office smash. Critics and audiences alike loved it.

Making movies is a tough business, which is why I prefer to work, whenever I can, with people I can connect with in an authentic way. I get excited about collaborating with someone not just because I respect their talents, but also because I sense that the perspective and intention they bring to the work will make the project better.

When I finished watching the HBO television series *The Night Of*, I knew I had to meet the lead actor, Riz Ahmed. In this haunting crime drama from writers Steve Zaillian and Richard Price, both of whom I'd worked with in the past on two of my movies (Steve as the writer of *American Gangster* and Richard as the writer of *Ransom*), Riz delivers a mesmerizing performance. I was awestruck by the transformation he was able to achieve as Nasir Khan, an American Muslim railroaded by the criminal justice system. At the start, Nasir comes off as gentle and naive. But after he is sent to prison, he is forced to adapt to life behind bars. By the end of the story, the innocent, doe-eyed boy becomes a hard-faced, streetwise man. John Turturro, who plays Nasir's lawyer, delivers a line to the jury that sums it up perfectly: "What I see is what happens when you put a kid in Rikers and say, 'Okay, survive that while we try you for a crime you didn't commit.'" For his performance, Riz, who is British Pakistani, made history twice over, becoming the first actor of Asian descent and the first Muslim to win an Emmy in a leading role.

Sometimes I read about someone—an actor, writer, director—or see their work and reach out to them about a specific project. Other times, there is no existing project. I will set up a meeting with an artist just because their talent struck me and I want to better understand who they are and what they're passionate about. Connecting with them gives me a chance to decide whether they are someone I'd like to collaborate with in the future, and in getting to know them, I get a better sense for what kinds of projects might grab them or be a good fit. The meeting I planned to have with Riz was this second kind.

As you have probably guessed by now, I have had thousands of meetings in my life with all different people who communicate in all different ways. Some of them have been easy to get to know. Others are naturally more difficult to connect with. There are certain people who can close the door on you even when you are focused, attentive, and asking good questions; they might respond with a one-word answer or look generally uninterested. For this reason, I always try to go into meetings (and curiosity conversations) with some background about the person with whom I'm sitting down, and some knowledge of topics that might be stimulating or relevant to them.

While this type of preparation may seem forced, I see it as necessary work for nurturing a relationship. When I enter a meeting with a potential collaborator, I always assume they are wondering, *What does this person have to offer me? What can he add to the conversation? Where do our shared interests lie?* Everyone sizes someone up before going into business with them. If I am fluent in another person's areas of interest, they are more likely to feel that I understand them on some level. That feeling of *Oh my gosh, I relate to you. I get it! I feel that too!* is what often ignites the desire to collaborate—in both directions.

Before meeting with Riz, I did my homework. What I learned is that being a talented actor is just one of many things that make Riz a superstar. He has also channeled his creative and intellectual energy into tackling racial profiling, lack of diverse representation in the media, and anti-immigration rhetoric.[11] As a student at Oxford, Riz had felt like an outsider among the wealthier white crowd. He managed to break into the black-tie social circuit by starting a weekly "club" night, at which he was the MC. It became one of the most popular events at the university and kicked off Riz's music career. Today "Riz MC," as he is known to his music fans, is half of a critically acclaimed hip-hop group called the Swet Shop Boys, which uses irreverent humor and sharp satire to protest social injustices. Riz, who also advocates on behalf of Rohingya and Syrian refugee children, was named one of *Time*'s "100 Most Influential People" in 2017.

Riz chose a small, unassuming restaurant on the west side of Manhattan for our meeting. When he walked in, his distinct energy and presence was palpable. I knew right away that he would have something of substance to say. As we started to talk, I looked into his soulful eyes, and I could feel the enormous power of his humanity. Infuriated by the world's indifference to the plight of refugees, he made a passionate and cogent case for why we need to stand up for these people, who like any of us, are just trying to survive and make a better life for themselves and their families. "We're all in this together," Riz said.

Before we even had a chance to talk about creative work, I felt connected to Riz. I was attracted to his spirit and certain that we could create something meaningful together. A project did in fact arise. Unfortunately, because of a competing commitment, Riz ended up having to bow out. There's no other way to put it—I was heartbroken. This wasn't the first time a project with someone didn't work out, and it wouldn't be the last, but I took this one especially hard. Riz had offered a bridge to a kind of authentic humanity and selfless purpose that isn't always easy to come by in Hollywood. I do believe in kharma, the kind where good things are born from pure intentions, and have a good feeling we will work together in the future.

Although it might sound counterintuitive, the best professional decisions I make tend to be the ones based on personal connections. If I trust in someone, if I am impressed and inspired by them, whether or not there's empirical evidence, then I am willing to take the chance that the other pieces will fall into place.

In the early 1980s Eddie Murphy was on fire. He made his big-screen debut in *48 Hrs.* with Nick Nolte in 1982. The following year, he appeared in *Trading Places* opposite Dan Aykroyd. And the year after that, he starred in the megahit *Beverly Hills Cop*, which in 1984 was the highest-grossing comedy of all time. I was dying to meet him.

In 1987 I got my chance. That year, Eddie was touring with his tremendously popular stand-up concert, *Raw.* (As of 2019, *Eddie Murphy Raw,* the live-audience recording, is still the number one stand-up film of all time.) Eddie invited Michael Keaton to the show, and Michael, whom I knew well from making *Night Shift* together, invited me. After the performance, we went backstage. I remember waiting a long time for Eddie to emerge. But when he did finally come out, he did it in fabulous fashion—decked out in a now iconic purple leather suit. He was well worth the wait. Eddie had a gigantic presence and magnetic charisma. Everything about him was shocking, original, and brave. He radiated a brash confidence and, even offstage, was brilliantly funny. You couldn't help but like him.

At the time, Eddie had an exclusive producing and acting agreement with Paramount. But I got the sense that the studio and Eddie were politely fed up with each other. Eddie had lost trust in the system and felt underutilized.

Experiencing his dynamism in person that night after *Raw*, I was more excited than ever to understand who Eddie was as an artist and a person. I called Skip Brittenham, the powerful entertainment attorney who repped him (who also happens to be my neighbor and tennis partner), and asked him to arrange a meeting.

With Hollywood stars like Eddie, many people—even big directors and high-powered executives—avoid making eye contact. I wasn't going to make that mistake. Sitting across from him, I leaned in and caught his gaze. *Who*, I wanted to know, *was the real Eddie Murphy? What really mattered to him?* He had a sharp antenna for disingenuous intentions. But from the look in my eye, my body language, and my tone of voice, Eddie could tell that I didn't want anything from him. He gradually opened himself up to a connection, and out of that initial sit down, a friendship began to develop.

As we got to know each other, it became clear that Eddie and I had the same goal: to create the highest caliber movies with the very best stories. Eddie, being a true savant across multiple art forms—comedy, music, and film—had endless ideas and we would spend hours talking through them. One day, Eddie shared an idea for a movie that eventually became *Boomerang*.

In *Boomerang*, Eddie plays Marcus, a hotshot, cocky advertising executive with a reputation for being the ultimate player and chauvinist. At one point, he has his assistant send flowers to nine different women with a card that reads "Only thinking of you." When a company merger places him under a beautiful new boss, Jacqueline, played by Robin Givens, Marcus sets his sights on her. Marcus and Jacqueline become involved and he quickly realizes that she is a female version of himself—noncommittal and conniving. Suddenly *he* is the subject of gossip at the office, and all the finger-pointing and snickering is about *him*. For the first time in his life, he is the one who gets played. It was a prescient idea; in the early nineties, movie and television plots were often centered around the male "player" as the person of power, and the woman as the one getting hurt. Now the tables were turned.

Our cast, which included Halle Berry, Chris Rock, Martin Lawrence, Eartha Kitt, John Witherspoon, and David Grier, was vibrant and talented. *Boomerang* was a hit and went on to become a cult classic. Over twenty-five years later, people still laugh about their favorite scenes and quote their favorite lines: *When I seduce you . . . if I decide to seduce you, don't worry. You'll know.*

Several years after *Boomerang,* Eddie and I made another comedy together. The movie *Bowfinger* was already under-way with Steve Martin, who wrote the script and named it after his favorite bistro in Paris. Steve had created the role of lead action star, Kit Ramsey, with Keanu Reeves or Johnny Depp in mind. But I thought, *This should be Eddie! He would be so brilliant as Kit!* I asked him to take a look. Eddie ac-cepted the part immediately . . . and thought it would be in-teresting and challenging if he played two roles. Not only did he want to play Kit, he also wanted to play a new character—Kit's look-alike, Jiff. Steve loved the idea, so we went with it.

To date, I've made five movies and a television series with Eddie that were all either creative or artistic successes, or both. None of it would have happened without an initial connection between two human beings. The most success-ful creative relationships—like any good relationships—start from a place of authenticity and pure intentions. This means showing up in our truth, with no ulterior motives, a genuine curiosity about the other person, and respect. When two people approach each other in this way, the outcome is almost always valuable for everyone involved. That first face to face between Eddie and me led to a deeply trusting relationship in which we see and bring out the best in one another.

These days in Hollywood, many studios, media platforms, and networks create algorithms and financial models that they hope will produce low-risk, breakout hits. As executives try to come up with a perfect formula to satisfy the audience at the lowest possible cost, story and character development can suffer and a project can quickly lose its soul. In this system, it's easy for an artist to get broken down.

For me, the most predictable path to creating a hit show is to build and nurture true and trusting relationships. With any artistic collaborator, whether the actor, the writer, the composer or another creative, I make it my goal to get to know them as a person and to understand what they want to communicate and why. If I find I can trust in them, I give them the space, freedom, and support to express what they feel in an honest way, from the soul. This lifts up the artist and, more often than not, results in storytelling that ignites a powerful emotional response in viewers, which is the ultimate goal of any film or piece of art.

CHAPTER 5

Trust in the Vision

*"Your vision will become clear only when you
can look into your own heart. Who looks outside,
dreams; who looks inside, awakes."*

—Carl Jung

People ask me all the time how a good movie is made. What *really* happens behind the scenes? They're usually interested in the juicier parts about stars and parties, so I'm never quite sure how to answer. The truth is that movies are often much less glamorous than people think. In fact, underneath all the polish, they can be unbelievably complex and challenging to bring to fruition.

As a film and television producer, my job is to nurture a creative idea from inception all the way through to its realization on-screen. Being a producer is very much like being an entrepreneur starting from zero every time. There are no guarantees and countless obstacles. It's a risky business. For each new project, you need to build a strong case that will be attractive to everyone from funders to actors to audiences— all kinds of people with different mind-sets, different concerns, and different ideas. Needless to say, it requires *a lot* of negotiation. Given all this, there are two things that are absolutely crucial for me to see a project through successfully—a clear and compelling vision that I believe in and the ability to form strong connections with others.

The idea for a film or television show can come to me anywhere at any time. Sometimes it is rooted in something personal; sometimes it's about an overarching universal human theme. Two of my first movies—*Splash* and *Night Shift*—were very personal to me. They were therapeutic at a time when I was a single twentysomething trying to work out things in my life. My futile search for true love inspired *Splash*, a rom-com (romantic comedy) about a man falling in love with a mermaid. The idea for *Night Shift* was born out of my almost superhero-like ability to get almost any job . . . and then lose it. I thought, *What would be the worst possible job that I could find myself in?* A night shift worker at a morgue running a prostitution ring seemed like a terrible— and hilarious—answer.

Whatever the idea, I ask myself some important questions about the story at the onset: *What is at the center of the story—a concept, character, theme, mission, or deep personal passion? What thoughts or feelings do I want the story to stir up for my audience? Why would they be drawn in by it?* But perhaps the most important questions are: *Why does it exist?* And *Why does it matter to me personally?*

A Beautiful Mind told the story of John Nash, a schizophrenic who earned a Nobel Prize in economics. I made the film to help destigmatize mental disability, or any kind of disability. It was a mission that mattered to me deeply. My son Riley, now thirty-two, has autism spectrum disorder. Back in elementary school, I was watching him from the fence and saw a bunch of kids hide his lunch tray while he was getting a drink. He came back to the table and was disoriented and confused as they all laughed. It broke my heart in pieces, and I wanted to do something about it. I was determined to tell a story that would be a vehicle to create empathy and compassion for those who are different.

Author Simon Sinek, who delivered one of the most watched TED Talks of all time, says, "People don't buy what you do; they buy why you do it. And what you do simply proves what you believe."[12] Making a movie or a TV show is not a solo affair. It takes studio backing, financiers, and a whole team of committed people—writers, directors, actors, production— working together. If I don't believe in the vision, or I can't articulate it in a compelling and persuasive way, then how can I expect anyone else to believe in it or commit themselves to it? How can I attract the most talented and interesting people to the project?

Sometimes, I'll come across a script or book I love for its plot or characters, but the message or purpose of the story is not immediately apparent or compelling to me. When that's the case, I will often try to find out what the writer intended, or work on it together with the writer until I truly believe in the vision. If I don't believe in it, then I don't want to do it. Because I know that no one else will believe in it, either. They'll just go through the motions to make the movie. And it will be shitty. We've all seen those movies.

Finding people who share my vision and convincing them to come on board is only half of the equation, of course. I couldn't do either of those things effectively, let alone make a successful film, without trust. People have to trust that I am authentic and genuinely believe in the project. They need to trust that I am going to hold up my end of the bargain and I need to trust them to do the same. We need to be able to come together, face to face, look one another in the eye and know that we are in it together, willing to do what we have to do to see the film through. Whether or not you are able to build trusting relationships will make or break not only a movie, but pretty much any big idea that you want to bring to life. One of the most powerful examples of this from my own life is the backstory of how the movie *American Gangster* got made.

Nick Pileggi caught my eye in the early nineties. Nick was married to the late Nora Ephron, and the two of them were toasts of the town, more specifically, literary toasts of New York. Nora was a superstar screenwriter first and then became a director. Nick was a renowned journalist specializing in American crime. When he came to my attention, he had just co-written the script for *Goodfellas*, based on his nonfiction book, *Wiseguy: Life in a Mafia Family*, and would soon pen the screenplay for *Casino*, based on his book of the same name.

I was impressed by the scope of Nick's knowledge on twentieth-century crime, and enthralled by his ability to foster rapport with so many Mafia bosses and organized crime figures. Somehow, he—a journalist, no less—had gained enough trust to earn entrée into that usually impenetrable world. So, naturally, I reached out to see whether he would have a curiosity conversation with me. He agreed and suggested we have dinner at Rao's, an Italian restaurant in Harlem that was notoriously difficult to get into.

Since it first opened in 1896, Rao's has occupied the same corner of East 114th Street and Pleasant Avenue. It wasn't until the seventies, however, when owner Frank Pellegrino took the helm, that it morphed into a true New York landmark. After Mimi Sheraton penned a glowing three-star review in the *New York Times*, the demand for reservations at Rao's went through the roof. It was more than the ten-table (technically four-table, six-booth) hangout could handle. To deal with this newfound fame, Frank came up with the novel idea—a time-share system of sorts. He assigned each of his customers a regular night—some weekly, some monthly— and a table. The original eighty-five regulars essentially "owned" their tables for the night—even if they finished dining early, the table would not be reset—and for life. When an "owner" dies, their family often inherits their table. As a result, it's nearly impossible to dine at this New York establishment. Even the likes of Celine Dion, President Bill Clinton, Hank Aaron, and even John Gotti had to have an "in" to dine here.

When I walked into Rao's, I felt like I had walked straight onto the set of *The Godfather.* Christmas lights (that apparently stay up all year long) hung on paneled walls along with photos of Sinatra and Frankie Valli. It was unusually bright inside, with a jukebox along the wall and a bar at one end—dark-stained, oak-panaled wood with a red leatherette pad where Nicky the Vest (so-called because of his rumored collection of over a thousand vests) held court. Far from fancy, Rao's was a homey throwback with a rack for coats near the men's room. It was a place where everyone seemed to know everyone and knew exactly what they wanted to eat. (At Rao's you don't get a menu unless you ask for one, and asking didn't seem advisable.) I had no idea what to expect of Nick, or what he would be like, but the sense of familiarity and exclusivity of the place seemed conducive to establishing a genuine connection with him. I was happy he had chosen this spot to meet.

Just then, Nick walked in wearing a dark shirt and jacket. He was tall (about six feet), balding, and wore big, round, tortoiseshell glasses. There was an intellectual quality about him and a quiet, unaffected way that was compelling to me. Immediately, I liked this guy.

We sat down at a booth, and the conversation was effortless. It turned out we had a mutual and intense interest in each other's crafts and worlds. I was eager to talk about Nick's writing and learn more about the crime world he knew so well. I knew he could feel my sincerity and interest by the way I listened and asked questions that made him think. He was an animated listener himself and responded by telling the most entertaining stories; I would reciprocate with some of my own from Hollywood. We were both intrigued by the complex characters who became leaders of organized crime, and the personalities of the enforcers, or lieutenants, beneath them.

Deeply charming, I could easily see why gangsters would open up to Nick. Even in the rare times when he raised his voice to punctuate the punch line in a story, he didn't intimidate. He spoke openly and kept eye contact. The warmth of his eyes drew me in, but not all the way. At a certain point they were guarded. Of course, that made sense. Nick was talking about crime and the Mafia. Everything was confidential. I got the sense that this meeting was a kind of test. That he would be gauging how far he could go, how much he could say to me, whether or not he was going to continue the conversation or excuse himself. I intuited that he had very clear, inflexible values and boundaries, and I respected him for it.

Eye to eye all night, jumping from casual and funny to deep and intense conversation, we were simultaneously processing one another as the stories flowed. I felt a trust with him that I can't quite describe. I understood why it had seemed, from the moment he walked in, that Nick was beloved by every person in the restaurant that night.

With a final farewell and a genial handshake, Nick and I ended the evening agreeing to stay in touch. I could tell that it was not one of those empty "keep in touch" moments. Over an Italian family-style dinner and a bottle of chianti, we had created a bond that, in my experience, usually takes years to form. We both thoroughly enjoyed the conversation, and each other. I knew that we would see each other again. Every year or so after that, Nick and I would get together to have coffee.

It was ten years after Rao's that Nick reached out to me with some urgency. He called me to say he had a story that he thought could be a movie. He had read the *New York* magazine article "The Return of Superfly," written by Mark Jacobson. It was the story of Frank Lucas, the biggest and most powerful heroin dealer and gangster in America during the seventies.

Raised poor in rural North Carolina, Frank moved to New York in 1946, where he saw a quick way to make money. He started robbing bars and jewelers, becoming more bold and brazen with each ensuing crime. He quickly realized that dealing dope was how real money was made on the streets. Frank started earning his stripes by going against both the Italian Mafia and the black crime syndicate. To break up their heroin operations, he decided to go directly to the source— the poppy fields of Southeast Asia.

In a move that was both outrageous and risky, Frank flew to the Mekong Delta during the Vietnam War and made his way through the jungle to meet face to face with Luetchi Rubiwat. Rubiwat, known by the nickname "007," was a legendary Chinese drug kingpin, who controlled all the heroin in the Golden Triangle, which comprises the borders of Thailand, Burma, and Laos. Frank struck a deal with him to guarantee shipment of heroin directly into the U.S., cutting out the middlemen. And that's how he single-handedly modernized the heroin trade and ended up the head of the largest drug empire in America . . . at least for a while. Eventually Frank was busted: a forty-year Federal term and thirty-year state term.[13] He was released in just a few years though after providing cooperation that led to over one hundred arrests.

After reading about Frank, Nick was intrigued. He secured special permission to visit him in prison and spent time getting to know him. "I know this guy ran the narcotics things," Nick told me, "but there was also a charm. He and I got to be friendly and when he got out of prison, I said to Frank, 'You are a story.' By then, he trusted me totally and I trusted him. At this point, we hadn't really sold anything yet, and he said he needed money to pay the tuition for his kid at Catholic school. It was ten thousand dollars. So, I wrote him a check for ten thousand dollars. My wife, Nora, said, 'Are you out of your mind?!' "

I was riveted, and immediately asked to meet with Nick and Frank at my office in LA. Just days later, across a long, shiny oval table in our conference room, I first laid eyes on one of the most notorious gangsters in American history. You could tell he was a boss. He had a commanding presence and charismatic air about him that made his mythology almost instantly believable.

I have to admit that the idea of meeting with a ruthless drug kingpin—let alone going into business with one—was a bit nerve-racking. Frank had spent a fair amount of time in prison, most recently seven years for heroin trafficking, and though he'd never actually served time for any violent offenses, the man had admitted at least once to being a stone-cold killer, although he later denied it.[14] But my curiosity was greater than any qualms I had. My desire to learn more about Frank was insatiable. It would not let up, and I had to keep peeling back the layers to see what was there. *What would he be like? Would his story hold up face to face? Could it translate well to film? Where was the redemption in his narrative?*

Once they were both seated, Frank set his sights right on me. I held his gaze with a strong, discerning look as he began to tell his story. At one point, I leaned forward and asked point-blank if he ever killed anyone. Although he didn't exactly admit to murder, he did offer up a shockingly graphic description of events that took place, including acts of disturbing violence. At the same time, he was also telling me about his devotion to his family and his deep and abiding loyalty to his mother.

It hit me that Frank was telling me his story of survival. The story of a semiliterate black man who was able to teach himself not just how to survive, but how to be successful in the face of poverty and brutality. It was a story with a theme that was larger than the specific details of Frank's life. At the core of it was the American dream and the human capacity for resourcefulness. I knew I had to make this movie. No question. No thinking. I bought the story right there in that room.

Next we had to hammer out the terms of our agreement with Frank. Naturally, he was always after more money. Given who he was, maybe he was always going to be squeezing us a little, trying to extract as much as he could. I pointedly looked him in the eyes and directly stated, "Look, I have a very good record of getting movies made. Believing in me and believing that the movie will get made will create the most remunerative income stream to you. You'll get the option payment now, a purchase payment later, and then bonuses for performance." He signed the deal with us. And he ended up earning every single payment.

Nick, now eighty-five years old, recently reflected on that fateful meeting, where all three of us committed to the long road ahead and got into business together: "I never had a doubt about you, Brian, ever. You're the person who truly committed to the project. I don't know what Frank would have wound up doing. By committing yourself, flying us out, Lucas began to trust me because I said, 'We're going to get this thing made as a movie.'"

Now, Nick realized that a Hollywood deal doesn't necessarily mean that a movie actually gets made, but from getting to know each other, and thanks to that first connection at Rao's, he believed in me. And I believed in him. I knew enough about Nick's values that if he believed in this story, then it was going to be good. In fact, much, much better than good. What I didn't know at the time was that I was about to embark on making the most difficult movie of my career.

With Frank on board, my next step was to find the best screenwriter in the world. Nick and I were both convinced that Steve Zaillian, who had won an Oscar for writing *Schindler's List* and had written other Oscar-nominated screenplays, was the one. Through Nick's personal friendship with Steve, I was able to make contact and convince him to read the Superfly article. He didn't immediately bite. It took him six months to really focus, and another three years of me constantly calling him, explaining the vision, and sending him research materials, to get him to commit. But—finally—he agreed to write the screenplay. And once he did, he was all in.

In order for Steve to write the most authentic and captivating script possible, I knew that he and Frank would need to get to know each other. Frank barely trusts anyone, but he did trust Nick. And since Steve and Nick are friends, it made sense to have him serve as a liaison. I hired Nick to spend a few months helping writer and subject connect with one another. Eventually, Frank became reasonably comfortable around Steve, and vice versa. Frank illuminated the shadowy, gangster underworld for Steve and granted him rare insight into the power dynamics at play there. For his part, Steve, with some help from Nick, turned in a stunning script. Every word he had written was genius; all of his ideas were elevated: strikingly original and sophisticated, surpassing any of our expectations.

I now set out to create a list of master filmmakers to direct, and I started at the top: Ridley Scott. Director of *Alien*, *Blade Runner*, and *Gladiator*, Ridley agreed to read the script because Steve Zaillian wrote it and they knew each other well. Ridley flat out turned me down. He said he liked the era in which the film was set, but he couldn't do it. I then asked a few other directors, but none of them had a great take on the movie. We continued to develop the script and after almost a year, I went back to Ridley. Once again he said no; he was still unavailable. So I finally gave in. I hired a different director.

My next challenge was convincing Steve to trim down the script. The completed screenplay he had turned in was 170 pages . . . that's *fifty* pages more than the maximum a script should be. Anything over 120 pages gets too expensive to make. As originally written, Steve's script would have been a $150 million movie. In the early 2000s, that was an exorbitant amount. We had to cut the script to cut costs. Steve, however, felt strongly that it should stay as it was. I held my breath and took the bloated script to the studio. The studio firmly replied, "*No way.*"

At this point it was becoming extremely difficult to get this movie made. But once I have faith in a project, I am wholly committed to it. Regardless of any challenge to my vision, whether time, economics, scale, or relevance, I need to see it through to the end. That meant I had to get this script that I was in love with, for a movie that I deeply cared about and believed in, down to a budget that the studio would green-light. When I had exhausted all my other options, I knew that the only thing left to do was to fire the greatest and most accomplished screenwriter in modern film history. I told Steve I would have to let him go. Not surprisingly, he was upset with me, and I thought I had burned that bridge for life.

I found a writer, Terry George, who could also direct the film. He said he could cut the film down to 110 pages, which he did, and Universal Pictures (accountable to their owner, General Electric) finally gave the green light. They agreed to make the film for a budget of $80 million, just over half of the previous estimate. Unfortunately, to achieve the lower cost, we would have to remove the scenes to be shot on location in Southeast Asia, and to me, that was a deal breaker.

Frank's trip to the Mekong Delta carried extremely high stakes. That he went so fearlessly into such a dangerous situation in a completely unknown land was critical evidence of his will, tenacity, resourcefulness, and desperation. The trip was essential to the theme of the film and the authenticity of the story. There was no way I could look Nick Pileggi in

the eyes and say, "Yeah, I think it'll be great" with this piv-
otal part of Frank's life missing. Nick trusted me with our
shared vision, and I wasn't about to break that trust. So, as
difficult as it was to fathom at this point, I decided that we
were going to have to go back to the drawing board. I told
the studio that I could not make the film without shooting
in Asia.

I needed Steve back on the movie. He understood the
vision. And his work was incomparable. It took lots of apol-
ogizing and lots of pleading, especially when the studio was
refusing to green-light the budget we needed, but ultimately
his belief in the project prevailed. I would reestablish trust
with him and together we would figure out how to pull it
all off.

Around that time, I hired Antoine Fuqua, a stylish com-
mercial director who had recently directed Denzel Washington in his Oscar-winning performance in *Training Day*. In
my mind, Denzel was the only person who could play the
complex and multidimensional Frank Lucas. Denzel was intrigued, and because he trusted both Antoine and me (we
first met when he was up-and-coming and not yet a big star),
he said yes to the part. With one caveat. A man of moral-
ity, Denzel made it a condition of his involvement that we
include Frank going to prison in the film. He felt that the
audience should see Frank paying the price for his brutality
and criminality. Prison is also where Frank finds redemption,
cooperating with the authorities to help bring about the big-

gest crackdown on corruption in the history of the New York City Police Department.

American Gangster was a "two-hander movie," so to speak—meaning it had two key roles. Richie Roberts was the highly principled and determined DA who ultimately brought down Frank Lucas, and then, ironically, after going into private practice, was hired to be Lucas's defense counsel. From there, the two became friends. I had to get somebody just as talented as Denzel to play Richie. I approached Benicio del Toro with the role. In appearance, Benicio was not the most obvious choice (he is Puerto Rican, whereas Richie was a New York Jew), but he is such a powerful and convincing actor that I thought he was the right creative choice.

Now I was building the movie with Steve, Antoine, and two huge stars. Everything seemed to be coming together. But then, with just four weeks to go before shooting was scheduled to start, the studio suddenly fired Antoine. With $35 million already spent in preproduction, including period wardrobe and props, Universal Pictures deemed Antoine fiscally irresponsible. They didn't want to see how high the costs would go once production started. So they decided to pull the plug on the film and absorb the loss. In shock, I went right to the head of the studio, who politely said, "Brian, we adore you, but don't say the words 'American' or 'Gangster' to us ever again."

That night the pain of the shutdown really hit me. I loved everything about this movie—the era, the music, Frank's ingenuity, the universal theme of surviving and succeeding against all odds. I loved that it was simultaneously a gangster movie *and* a movie about the American dream. Grappling with the reality that it might not get made was tough. But the following morning, I got in the shower and said to myself, *I've already been deeply affected by this story. I believe in this film. Steve and Nick believe in this film and they are counting on me to get it made. Today, I'm going to restart* American Gangster. *I don't care what the studio says. I'm going to find the people I need and convince them.* I had no idea how I'd do it, but I knew I could. Twenty years before, I had been persistent enough to make *Splash*, an impossible mermaid movie. I wasn't about to drop this movie easily.

Three weeks later, I was serendipitously at a Hollywood party where Ridley Scott happened to be as well. I saw him across the room and immediately beelined over to him. This time I stopped, took a breath, and focused my eyes directly on his. "Ridley, I know you've said no on *American Gangster* several times in the past, but please, would you take another read?" To my surprise, he said okay. The way he looked at me made me think it might be different this time. I was so hopeful, I started to meditate on it. It was all I could think about. *When is Ridley going to call?*

Within the week, he called. He said, "I'll do it. I'll make the movie. Do you think your friend Denzel will come back?"

I said, "One hundred percent." Of course, I didn't know, but I had to say so—and I had to believe he would. Everything was on the line. I immediately went to meet with Denzel. He respected Ridley's work and had had a great experience working with his late brother, Tony Scott. Most important, he still believed in the vision for the movie.

Denzel was back, but I still had to get somebody to play Richie Roberts, as Benicio had committed to another movie. Who else had his creative force? While making *A Beautiful Mind* with Russell Crowe, we developed a relationship of strong mutual respect. I knew he would be incredible as Richie. But how to convince him was another story. The role of Richie Roberts in *American Gangster* wasn't nearly as remarkable as the lead in *A Beautiful Mind* or *Gladiator.*

Russell and I met up to discuss the part. Having already read the script, he looked at me intently and he said, "The character is undeveloped; it's not there right now." I wasn't surprised; not only brilliant and well-read, Russell is also extremely street-smart. I knew him to be vigilant in pushing to make a better movie. I looked back at him and said with conviction, "We'll get it there. I'll dedicate myself to getting it there. Trust me—I'll use all my time and energy and resources to make it happen with you, and to fulfill this promise."

I shared my vision and belief in the story and told Russell that Steve Zaillian would work with him to create dialogue and a character that he could personally believe in. I was asking Russell to take a huge risk in committing to a movie before the character was acceptable to him. The fact that he took it was a testament to the trust that he had in me, trust that I had started to build during our first project together. Now Denzel and Russell, two of the most respected actors in the industry, were on board for the leading male roles.

Just when I thought we were actually ready to shoot, we hit yet another snag. The studio has a green-light committee that approves a film's budget, and it's a one-time event, no negotiation. They had approved the new iteration of *American Gangster* for $112 million—but Ridley Scott kept insisting it would cost $120 million. We had come this far, so I wasn't about to let a small percentage in the budget derail the movie.

I invited Ridley to my office, and when this strong, fearless, uncompromising director (he is known as "the General" for a reason) sat down on the L-shaped couch, instead of sitting catty-corner to him on the couch, which is what I would ordinarily do, I sat on the coffee table directly in front of him. With our knees touching, I looked at him and said, "Ridley, please listen to me. The studio's green-light committee will only allow us to start if we agree to the $112 million." This time, I was able to get through to him and he agreed. We were finally in business!

(Ironically the movie cost $120 million in the end. After agreeing to the original $112 million, Ridley later gave the studio the option for additional shots. They wanted those shots in the movie and so agreed to the higher budget. Funny how these things work out sometimes.)

Since we were filming in Manhattan, I decided to relocate my entire family to New York for one year, new schools and all. I've produced almost one hundred movies, possibly more, and I've never done that for a project; I knew I could better control films by *not* doing that. But this was a project where I had a pact with five people who were important to me—Nick, Steve, Ridley, Denzel, and Russell—and I was going to honor that pact. Being present in New York would serve as a reminder of the commitment we had all made to *American Gangster.*

Making it in Hollywood is like flying a Cessna through the fog. You often can't see where you are, but you have to keep going if you want to maybe arrive safely someday. Being a producer is far from a straightforward art or science. There were a million reasons why *American Gangster* should never have seen the light of day. But it did get made. In fact, it received many nominations and awards and went on to become one of the top-grossing gangster movies of all time.

I am convinced that the reason *American Gangster* exists is human connection. I never would have met Frank Lucas had it not been for that agenda-free dinner at Rao's with my now longstanding friend Nick Pileggi. And Frank would never have trusted me or Steve to tell his story if he hadn't first established trust with Nick. I am sure I would not have been able to get Ridley to direct had it not been for the goodwill we had developed prior to any movie and the trust he had in Steve as a scriptwriter. Denzel would not have been attracted to the project had he not had trust in me and Antoine. And so on. Through trust in each other and a tenacious belief in a shared vision, we brought *American Gangster* to life despite every challenge that came our way.

In some ways, there is nothing comparable to making a movie. But in other ways, I think it's like any other big undertaking. If the principal of a school wants to roll out a new student-leadership program, they must sell their vision to the students and teachers whose collaboration is imperative. A product manager for a new app must be able to articulate the product vision with passion and conviction, and then work cross-functionally with developers, finance, marketing, and sales to deliver it. A restaurant owner can only execute a new concept once they understand the story they want to tell.

Whatever business you're in, getting from idea to reality usually takes a group effort. And the best efforts are made when the group trusts in the vision and in each other.

CHAPTER 6

What Do Your Eyes Say?

*"You are responsible for the energy that you
create for yourself, and you're responsible for
the energy that you bring to others."*

—Oprah

Hierarchy is alive and well in Hollywood. The creator, executive producer, or showrunner (essentially, the lead writer) of a program is the most powerful and valued person in the television ecosystem. In the movies, it's the creative producer, or producer, who nurtures the idea to life and has the most decision-making power. In either business, you *start* at the bottom of the food chain—in the mail room, fetching coffee on set, or like I did, driving papers all over town for signatures. Even if you have insane writing talent, rarely can you just break into the industry. You have to work your way up and be willing to put in the time. More often than not, making a name for yourself takes patience, persistence, luck, and a clear understanding of who is in charge.

Despite this rigid power structure, there are those individuals lower down the ladder who seem uniquely capable of getting Hollywood to pay attention. They're not the producer, director, or top executive in the room, but somehow they are able to signal that what they say matters. Some will say ego plays a big part in it. But I believe that eye contact is the real key. A big display of ego easily comes across as arrogance or pretention and can put people off. In contrast, the right kind of eye contact can be magnetic, a powerful source of attraction. It is essential for asserting presence, projecting confidence, showing your humanity, and connecting with others—all qualities that in my observation make a person stand-out as unique and worth my attention.

Julie Oh is a talented young executive in our movie pod (a new structure we created at Imagine to work against the entrenched hierarchy and encourage a more entrepreneurial spirit) who demonstrates exactly these characteristics when she pitches me an idea. Her pitches are always impassioned and buttoned up. She communicates her resolve about a project with confident, unflinching eyes and keeps her gaze on me throughout our conversation, so that she can see whether she's reaching me. If I'm fidgeting or look confused or unconvinced, she pauses to ask whether I have a question or comment. When we encounter someone like Julie, who has (or appears to have) confidence, we're naturally attracted to their energy and want to hear what they have to say.

Many people that I've met in the highest positions of power have mastered eye contact so distinctly and skillfully that I absolutely believe it has helped them achieve their status. Leadership isn't always about strength, position, or circumstances. Being a great leader starts with looking people in the eye. After all, if you can't connect with people, you can't convince people of your beliefs. If you can't convince people of your beliefs, they won't follow you. If they won't follow you, you can't become a leader. Eye contact matters.

In 2005 I went to the White House to premiere the movie *Cinderella Man*. While I'd been to the White House before, this was my first encounter with President George W. Bush. I had no idea what to expect. He'd always presented as likable, with easy, Texan sensibility and style, but I didn't know what this would amount to in person. Would he be friendly or obligatorily polite? Would my conversation with him just be pro forma, like with other politicians I've met or know of?

The presidents I'd met to date had certainly impressed me. Bill Clinton, for example, really is as charismatic in person as his reputation suggests. He has a way of making you feel singled out even in a crowd. When I met him, I was struck by the sheer intensity of how he seemed to focus on just me. He looks straight at you, zeroing in on you with his eyes, making you feel the full weight of his interest in you and you alone. It's like being hypnotized. Even if you wanted to resist it, you wouldn't stand a chance.

Barack Obama, whom I first encountered in his office in Washington, DC, on the very same day I was to meet George W. Bush, had a completely different way about him. At the time, being a junior senator from Illinois, he was far from the height of his achievements. As the person who was ninety-ninth in seniority as a member of the minority party, he had the smallest office, situated farthest from the Senate floor. Still, you could feel the energy, purpose, and intensity in his eyes. Even though his office was the most crowded one I'd ever seen—it was jam-packed with his constituents, people spilling out into the hallway, carrying manila envelopes or bags of groceries—Obama seemed fully present for our conversation, completely engaged in a way that seemed almost, but not quite, relaxed. I could feel a certain deliberate edge. Not quite a calculation—he wasn't sizing me up—but rather a slight and subtle caution, perhaps just the natural outgrowth of his status as a politician.

So here I was at the White House to meet with George W. Bush. When we shook hands, I was stunned by how warm and inviting his eyes were. They were completely with mine, not rushing away. He was president of the United States, which meant he was incredibly busy. Yet his eyes signaled to me that he was fully present in the moment, patiently waiting to hear what I had to say. He came across as refreshing and completely unpretentious. He wasn't drilling into me or weighing my importance. He wasn't fishing for anything or trying to serve an agenda. He was just . . . with me, in a way that was altogether genuine.

Since he has a deep love for Texas, we talked about *Friday Night Lights*, which I filmed in Odessa, Texas. I shared what I had learned about that culture and he shared what it was like to grow up in it. As we talked, Bush maneuvered himself to my side so that we were standing shoulder to shoulder. Every time I would reposition myself to face him, he would immediately walk around to stand next to me again. Then he'd gingerly nudge up against me in a way that said, "Brian, it's all good." He didn't do it to avoid looking at me—in fact, he turned his head in order to maintain eye contact. I got the impression that literally standing shoulder to shoulder was a way for him to connect in a more egalitarian way, even though he was the president.

Though we might think of making eye contact as a discipline or a good habit—one that we can all learn—not everyone's eyes communicate in the same way. Each of us has our own style that uniquely identifies us. Almost like a fingerprint. The indelible mark of who you are. Clinton, Obama, and George W. Bush were all leaders of the free world, but they each have their own way of applying eye contact. In each case, how they look at you tells you something about who they are or who they want to be as individuals and in relationship to others.

When people look you in the eyes, they almost instantly decide whether they want to hear what you have to say, whether they trust you to be their leader, or whether they want to know you better. So it's worth reflecting on what your eyes are saying. Are they conveying what you want to convey? If you're warm and welcoming, do your eyes convey that? Does it take more time for people to get to know you because your eyes say something different than you intend? If you're not sure what your eyes are communicating, ask a family member or good friend how you come across. Then practice and adjust until the message you're sending with your eyes reflects who you are, who you want to be, and how you want to show up in the world.

We were deep into casting on my television series *Empire*—a show full of drama, conflict, bling, and very catchy music—and looking for "Cookie." Cookie Lyon is the outspoken wife of the show's protagonist, Lucious Lyon, a former drug dealer turned hip-hop titan. The storyline of *Empire* goes like this. After seventeen years in prison for taking the fall for her husband, Cookie gets released. She will stop at nothing to claim her half of their multimillion-dollar recording empire—an empire that Lucious had built in her absence using four hundred thousand dollars from the drugs she sold before her conviction. Meanwhile, all three of their sons are vying for the position as head of the company, so they wage war for control of *Empire* (think William Shakepeare's *King Lear* in the world of hip-hop).

As the family matriarch, Cookie is a complex character who shatters the stereotype of what a black, female ex-convict should be like. She is a take-no-prisoners hustler, but an immensely stylish one, with faith, humanity, and at times, deep compassion. She's a fierce, intelligent, loving force of nature. A charmer who is ferocious and flawed. When casting for her role, we looked for someone who could embody all these things. We wanted someone who had the strength and footing to challenge Lucious, but who would also possess a smart and bold femininity that audiences weren't accustomed to seeing. Just minutes into Taraji Henson's audition, we knew that she *was* Cookie. We immediately offered her the role.

I didn't meet Taraji in person, though. Not right away, and not for a while. I saw some of the first dailies—the unedited, raw footage—from the pilot, and simply from that I could feel the truth and potency of her presence. Her wide and sultry dark eyes were ablaze with force and intensity one minute, gentle and concerned the next. Cookie is always on the move, creating some kind of drama or situation, jumping from one show-stopping scene to the next with complete ease. Her energy has an explosive quality that is completely addictive to watch. Her "no filter" mouth says exactly what she wants, leaving zero room for misunderstanding. In the pilot episode, Cookie emerges from jail dressed in an eye-popping leopard ensemble and struts into the Empire record label offices. She belts out, "I'm here to get what's mine." She doesn't need to prove her worth, she demands the respect of everyone around her. When she swaggers into a room, you *feel* her. If you've seen *Empire*, you know exactly what I mean. Taraji embodies Cookie in a way no one else could.

Draped in fabulous furs and drenched in attitude, Taraji brought Cookie to life in a way that was much bigger than the character was written. Bursting out of the confines of the show, she was alive in social media, and celebrated on magazine covers, blogs, and talk shows. Women admired her: She's loud, savvy, wise, humorous, extremely blunt, unapologetic—and a feminist. I mean, what's not to love? *Vibe* magazine described her as "fierce, caring and extremely powerful. Her wardrobe is filled with fur, animal prints, gold and sparkles. After only one premiere show, women are asking how to look like Cookie."[15] Cookie had permeated the culture.

A few months after the show debuted, Taraji and I were able to find time to get together. I was excited and curious about what she would be like in person. It's rare to meet an actor whose style and persona off-screen much resemble their style and persona on-screen. Taraji is an exception to the rule. As soon as I saw her walk into the room, I knew immediately that she *is* as big of a presence in real life as her character is on the show. Maybe even more so. She radiated a kind of compelling energy that attracts your attention.

"I'm Brian," I think I said. Honestly, I don't know what I said. She has an unmistakable fearlessness in her eye that nearly took me off-balance. I caught myself by quickly referring to a technique in my head that helps me regain composure. I have a few of these techniques, and in this situation, I thought of a rubber band snapping my wrist. This visualization jolts me back to the immediate present moment (I've used it when meeting powerful politicians and heads of state, too). It allowed me to regain my footing so we could continue our conversation.

Taraji is whipsmart, creative, and gregarious, a straight-talker who, like Cookie, doesn't hesitate to tell you what she really thinks. I don't see her as someone who ever vacillates. And I found her immensely witty; she's quick to the joke and fun. We were able to establish a real connection that day, one that has since evolved into the great relationship we have now, one grounded in mutual trust and respect.

CHAPTER 7

It's Universal

"That's what storytellers do. We restore order with imagination. We instill hope again and again."

—Walt Disney

"Tell me a story!" It's something we have all said or heard from our kids at some point in our lives. Stories are as old as the rock drawings of the caveman and as modern as movies like *Black Panther* and the *Star Wars* franchise, which use cutting-edge CGI (computer-generated imagery) to create new worlds. Stories make life infinitely more interesting. Through them, we can even pretend to be someone else or escape to someplace far away. We can even do the impossible, like fall in love with a mermaid or travel through time. Stories contain lessons that open up our hearts and minds. They confer plausibility on everything from faith and science to love.[16] In stories, we find meaning.

As human beings, we are social creatures, and one of the most powerful tools of connection we have is a well-told story. Stories not only give us a reason to interact and engage with others, but they are also how we learn about ourselves, others, and their experiences of the world. We share stories wherever we go, when running into a friend on the street or gathered around the dinner table. We remember stories and they tie us together. It gives me a deep sense of fulfillment when people tell me how much a story in one of my films or in my first book, *A Curious Mind*, resonated with them and made them feel validated or not alone.

Of course, there is also a flip side to this. Stories are subjective. There are many ways to tell the same story, and infinite stories to be told. Not everyone is moved by the same stories, and not every story speaks to every person. This is one of the biggest challenges that the movie business, the television business, and any other business that trades in stories has—because the corporations financing media content (meaning TV, films, videos, music, and the like that are directed at the consumer), like most companies, are risk averse.

The paradoxical result of this conflict is that these story-driven industries are some of the toughest to break into for a storyteller with an original, creative vision. Which leads me to my point: If you want to make a living as a storyteller in Hollywood, you *must* learn the art of the pitch. And that art is all about making connections. None of my movies or shows would have seen the light of day if I hadn't been able to successfully pitch them.

The story or pitch meeting is a ritual that every writer, from the gazillion-dollar screenwriter to the lowly essayist, will sooner or later experience. Here's how it works. You come up with a movie or television idea, and go in and pitch it to different studios or potential buyers in order to get funding or distribution. It's a cutthroat environment. Studios sometimes hear thirty to forty pitches per day and select, at most, one or two. I am very familiar with the process. Even today, I continue to pitch stories I believe in. Alongside all my successes, I have endured countless rejections over the years.

When I wanted to make *Splash* I was turned down once, then twice, then so many times thereafter that I literally stopped keeping track. *No one* wanted a mermaid movie. I walked out of literally hundreds of meetings where the executives not only said no, but seemed to go out of their way to humiliate me by pointing out how stupid the premise was. I pitched *Splash* unsuccessfully for seven (yes, *seven*) years. Illustrating the definition of insanity to a tee, I kept on pitching it basically the same way—it was a mermaid movie— expecting a different outcome.

Then one day I had a conversation with a friend that changed everything. He asked me how I came up with the idea of a mermaid falling in love with an average, hardworking guy from Long Island. I told him that *Splash* was inspired by my personal search for love in Los Angeles, a place where everything—including relationships—seemed superficial. I started to fantasize about what my dream girl would be like ... *What if she were kind and generous? How would she look at me? What would it feel like?* Then I thought about how we would meet and what would make her unattainable. (Giving her a mermaid tail seemed like a sufficiently large obstacle.)

As I was talking, I stopped dead in my tracks. Suddenly I understood what I had been doing wrong in pitch after pitch—I had been trying to sell the studio execs on a story. But stories, as I've explained, are subjective. Anyone can argue against a specific story for any reason. It's much harder to turn down a universal theme, an experience, or feeling that almost every human being can relate to. With crystal clarity, I realized that I needed to reframe *Splash*.

My next pitch was with Disney. I went in and did everything differently. Rather than starting off by saying it was a story about a man who falls in love with a mermaid, I pitched it as a story about the universal search for love. Hasn't every person at some point felt that finding love was more elusive than meeting a mermaid? Would any one of the execs in the room dare to insist that love doesn't matter? I spoke with a conviction of personal experience that every other person in the room could relate to on some level. The studio finally bought *Splash*. Audiences loved it and I received my first Oscar nomination for co-writing the screenplay.

Now when I pitch a movie or television project, I always begin with an inarguable, universal theme, something that is essential to the human experience. My protagonists have goals that we all, as a species, want and root for—things like love, family unity, self-respect, and survival against the odds. Here are some examples.

Genius is a scripted docudrama series on National Geographic that dramatizes the stories of the world's most recognized thinkers and innovators. The first season of the show focuses on Albert Einstein. Ostensibly, we are telling the specific story of a single person—a rebellious young man, an unexceptional student, and unemployed father who unlocks the mysteries of the atom and the universe. But the pitch starts with the theme at the heart of the story: the struggle for self-realization and the courage to challenge established thinking.

A Beautiful Mind, as I mentioned in an earlier chapter, told the specific story of John Nash, a schizophrenic genius who earned a Nobel Prize in mathematics. Nash would've been destroyed by his disease had his wife's love not saved him. But here's the pitch: *A Beautiful Mind* is about anyone who is perceived as different. It's about taking up a more empathic lens and finding shared humanity.

Parenthood, a television series that tells the story of three generations of one family—the Bravermans—living in Berkeley, California, is really about the complexities and idiosyncrasies that exist within all our families. We all look across the street thinking the family over there is perfect, but what we come to realize is that none of them are. Similarly, while *Arrested Development* focuses on the dysfunctional Bluth family, it too is ultimately a celebration of love within families. However imperfect they may be, we want to see them stay together! Why? It makes us feel happy and secure.

I am convinced that this approach to pitches—looking for the common human thread in the story and opening with that—accounts in large part for my ability to "sell" my ideas in an ultra-competitive, high-stakes business that is generally wary of outside-the-box thinking. A universal theme increases the opportunity for the viewer to connect and relate to the narrative and is, therefore, the central ingredient in creating a transcendent event that brings the viewer to a heightened emotional state. That's what the best movies do, and when it happens, it inherently reduces the risk for the investor.

When you give the person you're pitching a theme that they can relate to and believe in, they will feel more connected to the story. But it is also absolutely crucial that they feel connected to you, the person doing the pitching. Over my many years of doing this, I've learned that it starts with being attentive and plugged in from the moment you arrive in the room. Rather than walk in reciting your opening in your head or tapping away at your phone, enter the room open and eager to establish a relationship.

Most meetings begin with a few minutes of small talk, but we've all been in that awkward situation where a few minutes threatens to continue on for eternity. The person leading the meeting doesn't know when or how to switch gears and you can see the other people becoming increasingly impatient. Try to get ahead of that impatience. Don't be afraid to take the reins of the conversation. You don't want to waste any more time than is necessary. In fact, I always ask, in a light and casual way, when the people I'm meeting with need to be out of there.

Even before you start to speak, let your eyes initiate the pitch. Be sure to direct your pitch *to* someone by catching their gaze. If you are pitching to more than one person, as is often the case, look at each person in turn. If you focus only on the most senior person in the room, others are likely to disengage. Given that the person in charge will usually ask for the opinions of the others in the room after you leave, keeping everyone engaged is highly advisable.

We've all had that excruciating experience when the people we're speaking to avoid our eye contact, glance down at their phones, or appear to glaze over. If you are attentive to your audience throughout the pitch, you will pick up on the signs that you are losing them early enough to reel them back in. This might require tightening up your story to focus on the highlights, or disrupting the moment with a quick, personal example—"For instance, yesterday I was talking with my daughter and she said a similar thing happened with her and her friends..."

Be aware that different people will react to your pitch in different ways and at different times. Their eyes, their body language (nodding, smiling, laughing), and their words ("That's so true!") will tell you whether it is sticking and with whom. More important, these signals will tell you when what you're saying is reaching their hearts as well as their heads.

Reading the audience throughout my pitch, I work to build excitement and momentum. When I can tell that everyone "gets it," I wrap up quickly. I always want to leave them wanting more. I don't try to force a decision on the spot or wade into logistics unless they take it in that direction themselves. If I already have other buyers interested in that show or movie, I simply say, "Let me know as soon as possible." Then I'm out.

Recently I have been working closely with my friend Malcolm Gladwell on a television series based on his bestselling book *Outliers*. The book seeks to answer the question: What makes high achievers different? "It is not the brightest who succeed," Gladwell writes. "Nor is success simply the sum of the decisions and efforts we make on our own behalf. It is, rather, a gift. Outliers are those who have been given opportunities—and who have had the strength and presence of mind to seize them."

The message of the book—that meeting opportunities with hard work is more important than intelligence when it comes to success—resonates with me on a deep, personal level and I have been enthusiastic about the collaboration. When I pitch the series, I'm not just selling something. I truly believe in it.

Just recently I had a pitch meeting with a decision maker whom I respect but find very hard to read. His demeanor is almost stoic, and he rarely offers a word to help you unlock what he's thinking. From the start of the meeting, I was uncomfortable. The room was dead quiet and the energy was completely flat. There was no buzz to tap into or build on. How was I supposed to whip up excitement for the project under these circumstances? There was only one way to find out.

I cast off any doubts and inhibitions I was feeling and flew into an impassioned case. I gave it everything, delivering my pitch authentically and with conviction. By the end, I felt confident that I had connected with everyone in the room— almost everyone, that is. I walked out of the room that day still uncertain as to whether I had forged a connection with the one person whose decision mattered most. True to form, he wore one of the best poker faces in the business through- out the pitch.

To my surprise, later that night, I received a rare call from the decision maker. He wanted to tell me how much my story had affected him. By tapping into my own passion for the project, I had managed to connect with this person who I'd only ever known to be dispassionate. Hearing that my pitch had reached him on such a profound level felt really good. Whatever he decided about the series, I still felt that I had succeeded. Life is about people, and when I feel like I'm con- necting with someone I deeply respect, it matters as much or more than selling a project. I find it deeply satisfying.

CHAPTER 8

In the Public Eye

"Courage is what it takes to stand up and speak;
courage is also what it means to sit down and listen."
—Winston Churchill

All of us have heard this question hurled at us at some point: *What are you looking at?* The fact is, not everyone wants to be looked at, or looked at by a certain person, or looked at in a certain way.

Back in my school days, when I didn't yet understand my learning disability, I was extremely self-conscious. It wasn't just my teachers that I didn't want looking at me. I didn't want *anyone* looking at me. If I thought I felt someone's eyes on me or caught them glancing in my direction, I would get defensive and lash out. This led to a fair number of altercations, earning me a reputation as someone who didn't turn down a brawl.

Consequently, it seemed like there was always someone who wanted to pick a fight with me. When I was fourteen, it was a tough kid from Texas—Jack Jones—who challenged me in the middle of the cafeteria, right in front of everyone (usually the custom was to meet out by the handball courts, where at least the audience would be a little smaller).

"Let's do it right now, man," he said, standing up.

As the other students turned to looked at me, I felt the heat rising up through my body. I didn't want to fight Jack. But I didn't feel like I had a choice, either. If I backed down, the others might think of me as a coward. If I didn't, chances were high I'd get my ass kicked.

"All right," I said. "Let's go." And indeed, I got my ass kicked.

Now that I'm an adult, I know that when we worry about what other people think, we are giving up our own power and that sometimes *not* giving in to insult or antagonism is the best way to convey our strength. I've also been able to shed the self-consciousness that plagued me as a kid, which is fortunate given that I now have a career that puts me at the center of attention nearly every day.

Today, whether I'm leading a pitch, speaking at a conference, on the set of one of my movies, or appearing on camera myself, I'm regularly in the spotlight with all eyes on me. There is one thing that has allowed me to find comfort there and even, most of the time, enjoy it: establishing intimacy with the audience through connection. But how do you create intimacy—a feeling much more easily achieved face to face—with an audience of dozens, hundreds, or even thousands of people?

Back in 2002, I was at the Oscar Nominees Luncheon at the Beverly Hilton Hotel alongside Will Smith. Will had been nominated for his performance in Michael Mann's film *Ali*, and Ron Howard and I had both been nominated for *A Beautiful Mind* (Ron for best director and both of us for best picture). The luncheon was a strange event: It was designed to be informal and relaxed. In reality, it felt more uncomfortable than the awards themselves.

You might imagine a ballroom full of Hollywood insiders who all know one another flitting from conversation to conversation with ease, swapping compliments and accolades, and generally having a good time. But the opposite is true. Many of us know each other by reputation only, and it's more than a bit intimidating to have the eyes of your most respected peers on you. Add in the unspoken awareness of competition (we are, after all, there competing for the same awards!), and it's no day at the beach. I was a little nervous just being at the luncheon, so I couldn't help but be impressed when Will Smith spontaneously stood up and addressed the room.

"Hey!" he said with a huge smile. "Isn't this a blast?! Aren't we all excited to be here?! It's great to see everybody!"

In that moment, one person single-handedly changed the entire dynamic of the room. By recognizing our shared uneasiness, Will connected with me and everyone else at the luncheon who thought they were alone in their discomfort. As Will spoke, we laughed and clapped away the tension. By the time he sat back down, the mood was lighter. Everyone had loosened up. More than Will's words—truthfully, I don't even remember most of what he said—it was his outgoing nature and carefree manner that made the difference. He was effervescent, the embodiment of ease and self-assurance. (You never would have known that he was the underdog that year, with *A Beautiful Mind* and *Training Day* favored to win over his own film.)

Now, you might be thinking: *Well, he's Will Smith. Of course he was charming and confident.* But I know lots of celebrities—many more than you'd think—who also appear to be sure of themselves, yet who are shy and uncomfortable when it comes to speaking in public or before a large audience. I have no idea how Will was feeling internally in that moment, whether he was uncertain or anxious. What I do know is there are few who would have taken the risk that Will did. It took courage to attempt to connect not just with a single person, but with a whole room full of people, not knowing whether or not they would be receptive.

When I have to speak in public, I remember how Will carried himself at that lunch and the way it transformed the mood in the room. We all know someone like that, I think: not necessarily someone famous, but someone who, for whatever reason, seems to have easy access to the most relaxed, least-rehearsed parts of themselves. As you prepare for a speech or presentation, it can be helpful to visualize that person. You might even picture them *while* you are speaking.

In your mind's eye, see how they stand, how they move, how they make you feel when they look at you. As you imagine them, don't imitate them, but try to internalize their presence and make it your own.

In 1996, our movie *Apollo 13* had been nominated for an Academy Award for best picture. In the weeks leading up to the awards ceremony, I'd been assured by many people that it was the odds-on favorite to win, and so while I won't say I "expected" to win, I certainly felt we had a good chance. Just in case, I'd taken my time to write a well-considered acceptance speech.

As I sat in the theater on the evening of the Oscars, I felt overwhelmed. Although it wasn't the first time I had been there, I was still affected by the knowledge that I was surrounded by nearly every important person in the business and part of a live broadcast that would be watched by a good thirty-five million viewers around the world. That's a lot of eyes. My pulse was definitely elevated.

I tried to stay calm, but when the time came to announce best picture—always the last award of the evening—I was on the edge of my seat, vibrating with nervousness. *Was this it? Were we going to win the Oscar?* Sidney Poitier, always a tremendously elegant and deliberate speaker with extraordinarily sharp enunciation, would read the winner. My anxiety was at an all-time high.

"And the Oscar for best picture is presented to . . ." Sidney opened the envelope. I clearly saw his mouth shape itself into a *B*. Since the producer is the one who goes up to accept the award for best picture, I immediately leapt to the conclusion that he was starting to say my name. *Brian,* I thought. *Presented to Brian Grazer!* I jumped excitedly out of my seat and actually started walking toward the stage.

"*Braveheart!*"

I stopped dead in my tracks. My entire body broke out into a hot sweat. I tried to sneak back to my seat unnoticed—walking backward in slow-motion—but of course people were cocking their heads back to look at me. A few rows away, the head of a major studio looked at me and held his thumb and index finger to his forehead in the shape of an *L*, the universal symbol for "loser." I was mortified! I collapsed back into my seat and sunk way down. It felt like the world was closing in on me.

I was on the aisle. Ron, who directed *Apollo 13*, was sitting next to me; and next to him was Jim Lovell, the astronaut played by Tom Hanks in the movie. Suddenly I felt Jim grab my arm. He leaned across Ron and looked me in the eye.

"It's okay," he said. "I never made it to the moon either!" It was a gracious thing to say, and it made me feel better. It grounded me.

Years later I was up for another Oscar. That night things were a little different. Even though the odds—again—seemed to favor *A Beautiful Mind*, I didn't want to take anything for granted. I had a list of names in my pocket—people to thank if we did win—and some light talking points, but not much more. I guess I didn't want to jinx anything by being too prepared.

The awards finally rolled around to best picture, and Tom Hanks walked out to present. There I was again on pins and needles. But this time I didn't move a muscle. The live camera flashes on each nominee as they're announced, so I kept a calm face—well, as calm as I possibly could. Tom opened the envelope. And then he said, "The Oscar goes to *A Beautiful Mind*, Brian Grazer and Ron Howard, the producers!" With adrenaline pumping through my body and everyone cheering, I got up and took a few steps. Russell Crowe hugged me and whispered a few encouraging words.

I may not have looked like it as I climbed up to the stage, but I was actually shaking. I wanted to give everyone who contributed to the movie some love, so I pulled the little piece of paper from my pocket and looked at it. But, as we all now know, reading is not my strength! I couldn't focus. Anxious thoughts ping-ponged through my head. *What if I tripped over my words, or spoke too long and got cut off by the music?*

At that moment, I looked up and scanned the crowd. My eyes found five actresses sitting in the front row: Angelina Jolie, Nicole Kidman, Renée Zellweger, Julia Roberts, and Sandra Bullock. I suppose that sounds like an imposing quintet—five women of astonishing talent, accomplishment, and beauty—but as it happened, I knew all of them. And by looking at each of them in turn, I was able to regain some degree of control. Just as Jim Lovell had in my less-triumphant moment, these formidable women—who also happened to be my friends and peers—were there to lend support. As I struggled to keep my list of names on my paper in order, I could see them rooting for me. Their eyes said *You can do it.* I broke off from my planned speech and made an off-the-cuff remark.

"I am *so* nervous," I confessed to the sea of people in front of me. "I know it's imperceptible."

It certainly wasn't. The audience laughed and the room opened up. It broke the ice for me completely. If I hadn't been able to connect with those familiar faces in the front row, who knows how things might have gone.

That night, I used a trick that has served me well in countless other public-speaking situations. I narrowed my focus from a giant group to an individual (or individuals in this case). That allowed me to establish an intimate connection under circumstances that were anything but. And that connection was my lifeline. This approach might sound simple, and my experience might seem a little rarified—not everyone has the terrifying good fortune to have to speak on live television—but the principle is the same no matter who you are or where you are speaking, be it at a sales meeting or at a birthday party.

A few months ago, Veronica and I asked our fourteen-year-old son Patrick to introduce us at the World of Children Awards, where we were being honored. Now, Patrick is a pretty poised kid, and it wouldn't have been obvious to most people, but as his parents, we could tell he was nervous about it. This would be his first time speaking in front of a crowd, and it wasn't going to be a small one.

On the night of the event, we were all sitting at a table up front. It was the entire family, including his aunt and uncle and many of our friends. I noticed that the ink on Patrick's note cards had been smudged by his sweaty palms. Then I heard him whisper to Veronica. He wanted to know whether he could quietly practice his introduction with her one last time. So sitting there at the table, they blocked out their surroundings and got focused. Veronica reminded Patrick to speak slowly, to take natural pauses, and most important, to look up and connect with the audience. She told him to find our faces in the crowd and he would feel us rooting for him.

The time came and Patrick walked up to the podium. Seeing him look so poised in my light gray suit and favorite skinny black tie, I started to tear up. Veronica and I watched him take a deep breath and scan the front row for us. As soon as we locked eyes, he felt safe and started to speak.

"I'm so glad that my dad and Veronica asked me to come up and say flattering things about them . . . in front of three hundred people!"

The audience laughed, and Patrick burst into a big smile.

He continued to speak slowly and surely, pausing, looking up, and smiling. He was a natural!

Sometimes you have to speak in front of an audience where the kind of personal connection I found at the Oscars and Patrick found at the dinner isn't available. In those cases, the next best thing is to *forge* a connection with someone in the audience. You might, for example, focus on the person directly in front of you and imagine you're speaking only to them. Or you might challenge yourself to find a way to get the attention of a particular individual in the group.

A few years ago I was invited to speak at the Microsoft CEO Summit outside of Seattle. The audience would include other invited speakers, including Jeff Bezos, founder and CEO of Amazon; Warren Buffett; Muhtar Kent, then CEO of Coca-Cola; Rex Tillerson, then CEO of ExxonMobil and former secretary of state; and Bill Gates himself. These were the business equivalents of the Hollywood elite I had been face to face with at the Academy Awards. And once again I found myself a little jittery. To make matters worse, before I went onstage to speak, I was warned by someone that Gates would be sitting in the front row. He had a habit, I was told, of checking his phone during these speeches. So even though he would be following along with my speech, it would appear that he wasn't paying attention to me. I shouldn't be offended; it's just how it was.

The gauntlet had been thrown down. If Gates was so hard to engage, I was determined to engage him. But how would I do it?

As it happened, Gates was up right before me. In his speech he mentioned that there were portions of the world where a dominant part of the population still contracts polio. Well, I seized upon this piece of information. Jonas Salk, who developed the first polio vaccine, was one of my childhood heroes, and meeting him had been one of the most important encounters of my life. Up onstage with Arianna Huffington, founder and CEO of Thrive Global and founder of the *Huffington Post*, interviewing me, I decided to tell the story.

"Bill," I began, "you mentioned polio, and I have to tell you, Jonas Salk was a hero of mine . . ."

That got his attention. He looked up and I caught his eyes. Even though I was on a large stage talking to a large audience, it was as if I were talking directly with Gates.

The story, which I also describe in *A Curious Mind*, went like this:

When I first started my curiosity conversations, Salk was among a short list of people with whom I had a fervent desire to talk. I was a nobody at the time, and he was one of the most famous medical researchers in the world. But I was persistent. I would call and write his assistant every week, regardless of whether I got a response. Finally, I caught my break: He got a new assistant. I still remember her name—Joan Abrahamson. Joan was a fresh start. She had no reason, yet, to be sick and tired of me and my desperate pleas to meet with her boss. I continued to call and send letters until Joan told me I could maybe meet Salk for a moment— nothing more—after he gave a talk at the Beverly Hills Hotel.

I was overcome with excitement and scared that I would miss my chance—that I would be late, get lost, or wouldn't be able to find the room. So I arrived at the hotel two hours early. After what seemed like a lifetime of waiting, I saw my childhood hero across the lobby. I began walking to meet him. With every step toward him, my panic grew. I moved closer and closer until I was finally face to face with him. Then, right as I was about to shake his hand, I threw up on him. I nearly fainted!

Dr. Salk knelt down beside me to see what he could do— he was, after all, a medical doctor. He cradled the back of my head and signaled the waiter for a glass of orange juice to stabilize my blood sugar. He may have been the man who cured polio, but he behaved as a regular doctor in that mo- ment. He looked in my eyes—and, however out of it I was, I managed to look back. We became friends and remained so until the day he died.

As I told the story, I made sure to keep my eyes on Gates. I couldn't help but notice that he didn't look down at his phone once.

CHAPTER 9

Listen Up!

*"When you talk, you are only repeating
what you already know. But if you listen,
you may learn something new."*

—Dalai Lama

I was set to have lunch with my old friend Jimmy Iovine. Jimmy and I have known each other for many, many years; in fact, we produced the movie *8 Mile* together. Jimmy is the co-creator of Beats headphones with Dr. Dre, but his career actually began as a recording engineer for John Lennon. He went on to found Interscope Records where he signed U2, Tupac, Lady Gaga, Gwen Stefani, Eminem, 50 Cent, and countless other recording artists. Jimmy is an icon in the industry. He's the type of guy who's very connected to the culture and seems to have a vivid and original insight on just about everything. He and I are close, so we get together whenever we can, and our conversations are always juicy and interesting.

One day we made plans to go to The Palm—a power-lunch spot in Beverly Hills owned by my friend Bruce Bozzi—and had decided to invite Mark Wahlberg as well. I've known

Mark, too, for a long time—I offered him his first leading role as an actor in a film I produced called *Fear*. He started his career as a recording artist with Jimmy at Interscope—so we all knew each other. It was shaping up to be a fun afternoon.

The morning of our lunch, I was sitting at the kitchen table when my phone rang. It was David Geffen. David is a legend, unprecedented in his successes in multiple artistic arenas—music, film, *and* Broadway.

"Brian, what are you doing?" David said. "Would you like to have lunch today?"

I've known David the longest of all—forty years. When Ron Howard and I produced our first film together, *Night Shift*, David had offered a powerful moment of validation when he stood up at a packed screening with the entire executive team and both chairmen of Warner Brothers in attendance and declared that he loved the movie. This single act gave both the film and my early career a tremendous amount of propulsion.

"I'm having lunch with Jimmy and Mark Wahlberg," I said. "You want to join us?" David and Jimmy are also close friends.

"Sure," David said. "That sounds great."

A few minutes later, I got a text from Jimmy.

Bono is coming.

Unlike the other guys coming to lunch, Bono wasn't someone I knew well, so I was excited for the chance to spend some time with him.

———

One o'clock rolled around, and David, Jimmy, and I arrived at The Palm first. We were seated at a cozy booth—my favorite one, actually. Then Mark and Bono arrived and squeezed in with us.

The booth was designed for four people, so we were packed in tight. Our legs were even touching. This immediately made the gathering more intimate than it would have been at a big table where everyone was spaced out. It was a set-up conducive to conversation and connection. I liked that.

Often, when I am spending time with really interesting people, I feel compelled to reciprocate. That's my habit when approaching curiosity conversations: to not only take, but give back right away with a story or gift of information. On this day, I decided on a different approach. Rather than dive headfirst into conversation, I concentrated on giving my full attention to the guys I was with. I wasn't mute, but I also didn't feel the need to return every story with a story.

I was especially interested in what Bono had to say. He is, after all, one of the most talented rock stars in the world, not to mention a dedicated humanitarian, whose work has touched millions of people living in extreme poverty and with HIV/AIDS. There was so much I wanted to ask him: *What is his unique view on the world? What's most meaningful to him? What's top of mind for him right now?* But I didn't want to disrupt his flow. So I limited my questions to a couple and focused on conveying my desire to know more through my eyes.

Although I knew some about Bono's work in Africa and around the globe, hearing him talk about it firsthand gave me a new and deeper understanding of its enormous scale. *Wow,* I thought to myself, *this guy is working on a higher purpose, at a higher level with all these governments to help alleviate poverty and AIDS.* I was impressed and moved. Even more than that, I was inspired.

Through my movies and work with nonprofits, I had long been doing purposeful work. But listening to Bono stirred up all kinds of new ideas about how I could use my own position, talents, and resources to effect positive change in the world. In fact, that lunch was one of the things that helped inspire my latest initative—a global content accelerator, called Imagine Impact.

The way Impact works is that thousands of writers from all over the world apply to participate in a boot camp of sorts, modeled after the famed Y Combinator start-up accelerator in Silicon Valley that made seed investments in Dropbox, Airbnb, Reddit, DoorDash, and many others. The twenty-five or so people chosen for Impact receive hands-on mentorship from the brightest and most accomplished creators in the industry. Once they have gotten their projects to the finish line, they are then given the opportunity to pitch them to Hollywood buyers. Godwin Jabangwe, a talented writer from Zimbabwe who had twelve dollars in his bank account, was selected for the first Impact class. He pitched his animated family adventure musical called *Tunga* and a four-way bidding war ensued. Netflix won and bought it for $350,000. The musical was inspired by the mythology of the Shona culture of Zimbabwe, a culture Godwin was raised in as a child. It tells the tale of a young African girl named Tunga, who, after the death of her father, must venture to a mythical lost city whose spiritual elders can teach her how to summon the rain and save her village from a terrible drought.[17] Impact not only gives writers like Godwin a chance to build careers in an industry that is notoriously difficult to break into, but also gives global audiences the chance to hear from new and important voices that we might otherwise miss out on.

I woke up that morning with just an easy lunch on my calendar. I could never have predicted where it would lead or what it would inspire.

Sometimes we need to participate equally in a conversation to make a meaningful connection. But not always. Listening can be just as powerful as talking, if not more, when it comes to establishing a bond with another person. When we are talking with someone, we often spend more time thinking about what we are going to say rather than we do paying attention to what's being said. Stephen Covey says, "Most people don't listen with the intent to understand; they listen with the intent to reply."[18] People feel valued when they are listened to, which fosters feelings of trust and respect. In return, when you give someone your full, undivided attention and show them that you want to hear more . . . they will usually give you more. This is especially useful to remember when you are entering a conversation that you are unprepared for or want to connect with someone whose base of knowledge is different than yours. We become wiser and more knowledgeable when we are willing to really pay attention. Good listeners give themselves opportunities to understand other people's viewpoints and widen their own. Not to mention, it's a differentiator; great listeners are not so common!

In 2004, Ron Howard and I purchased the film rights to the book *The Da Vinci Code*. Right around that time, I took my daughter Sage to see Prince in concert. He was playing a small, private show at a (now-closed) venue called Club Black in lower Manhattan, and I thought it would be fun for the two of us to see him together. I'd met Prince once before, just briefly. I was doubtful that he'd know who I was, let alone remember me.

Once Sage and I had passed the bouncers, we filed into the club, where Prince was standing at the door, greeting people. We were in line in front of various celebrities he seemed almost sure to know, people I imagined he would want to talk to. I expected we'd slip by with a cursory hello, but to my astonishment he actually did remember me.

"Brian, hi," he said. "It's nice to see you."

Like any father would be, I suppose, I was proud in that moment. I wanted to impress Sage, and, well, what could be more impressive than this? I wanted to hold Prince's attention, to prolong the moment a bit, so I held his gaze. It worked.

"What are you working on?" he asked.

I told him that I'd just optioned *The Da Vinci Code*. Why not? It was a famous book, a huge bestseller.

"Really?" he said. "Oh my God, that's amazing. I loved *The Da Vinci Code!*"

Now, it might have slipped my mind at the time—or maybe I hadn't known this before—but Prince was famously religious. He was, in fact, a devout Jehovah's Witness. *The Da Vinci Code* is steeped in alternative theories of religious history about things like the Merovingian kings of France and a marital relationship between Jesus and Mary Magdalene. I'd read the book before optioning the rights, so I knew a little bit about these theories, but I hadn't studied them in any depth. Prince, on the other hand, appeared to be an expert on all of it.

"Have you read *The Templar Revelation*?" he asked me. "Or *The Woman with the Alabaster Jar*?"

Had I read them? I'd never heard of them. I felt a little like a high school student who'd just been hit by a quiz he hadn't studied for. I didn't want to make a fool of myself, but I wasn't going to lie, either.

"I haven't," I admitted.

The longer I could keep the conversation alive, I thought, the more memorable it would be for my daughter. So I gave Prince the only thing I had to offer at this point: my attention.

I kept my eyes focused on his and said, "Tell me about them."

I didn't know anything about Pierre Plantard (a French draftsman whose theories about the Merovingians have been disproven) or anything about any of the other topics Prince was speaking about with such mastery. Yet I was able to hold the connection. With nothing more than my eyes and a few sporadic words of agreement, like "fascinating" and "tell me more," I kept Prince engaged and the conversation going. Behind me I could feel people getting impatient. I didn't care. Sage and I still talk about that epic night when one of the greatest artists of all time spent almost ten minutes bonding with me over conspiracy theories!

CHAPTER 10

Adapt or Die

*"Empty your mind, be formless. Shapeless, like water.
If you put water into a cup, it becomes the cup. You put
water into a bottle and it becomes the bottle. You put it
in a teapot, it becomes the teapot. Now, water can flow
or it can crash. Be water, my friend."*

—Bruce Lee

Maybe you swore off texting and driving, but couldn't resist that one last text that caused you to swerve, barely missing another car. Maybe you missed the opportunity to meet a new romantic interest because you were in the corner watching the game instead of mingling at your friend's party. Or maybe you've had the embarrassing experience of being called on to answer a big question at a meeting when you were lost in thought about plans for the weekend. If any of these has happened to you, hopefully you bounced back easily. The point is, it's easy to make missteps, have accidents, or miss opportunities when we're distracted. When it comes to communication, if we are not paying attention to the people around us—or face to face with us—we are more likely to miss out on key information, misunderstand intentions, and lose opportunities to gain or keep trust and respect.

If we want to have the kind of communication that leads to meaningful connections, it is essential that we stay alert and fully focused. For me, eye contact is key to being present. When I am engaged with my eyes, my mind is less likely to wander. If a conversation is falling flat—which does happen—and my mind starts to think about Jon and Vinny's arugula pizza, refocusing my eyes on the person I'm with pulls me back into the moment and centers me.

The Roman emperor Marcus Aurelius, sometimes called "the Philosopher," was known for his ability to focus and avoid distraction. Aurelius advised that the best way to concentrate is to imagine the task at hand to be the last thing you'll ever do. None of us wants our last living act to be sloppy or less than meaningful. Aurelius also believed that a simple mantra could bring focus, so you might want to think about creating your own personal one. Whatever mantra you pick, saying it to yourself before meeting someone, before a speech, or before an important project will help prime your mind to keep distraction at bay.

In a conversation, there's a constant flow of information—nonverbal information—that we can only glean from reading a person's eyes, expressions, and body language. So, when I am giving someone my fullest attention, I am able to absorb all sorts of data that otherwise would have been unavailable to me. Looking into someone's eyes, I can get a better feel for their emotional state. I can tell when their eyes light up that they are excited about what I am asking or interested in what I am saying. I can tell when they start to shift their eyes away from mine that they are uncomfortable with where things are going or are losing interest. All of these cues help me navigate the conversation and connect.

When I am fully attuned, I'm more likely to recognize and seize opportunities when they arise, whether it's a chance to engage someone new or deepen a relationship with some-one I already know. Likewise, the more attentive I am to the person in front of me, the better I'll be able to react and re-spond when the conversation begins to take an unexpected turn or the nature of the connection we are forming begins to change. This happens more frequently than you might expect. Over breakfast, a partner shares that he hasn't been happy in the relationship for a while. During a run-of-the-mill meeting, a co-worker you barely know reveals that you've always been her trusted mentor.

Here is one of those situations I remember clearly.

After watching *The Man Who Would Be King*, John Huston's film based on Rudyard Kipling's fantastic adventure story, I became curious about the ultrasecret society of Freemasons; all three of the main characters—Kipling played by Christo-pher Plummer, a traveling stranger played by Michael Caine, and Daniel Dravot played by Sean Connery—belong to this mysterious brotherhood that was rumored to be a managerial elite that controls the world.[19] I wanted to know more.

Many different orders and levels of Freemasonry exist, with the highest order called the 33rd degree of the Scottish Rite.[20] I was eager to meet the two men—a father and son who were the regional heads of the organization in the western United States—for a curiosity conversation. It took some effort, including a number of letters and phone calls to their office explaining my intentions, before they eventually consented to meet me.

On the agreed-upon meeting date, two older, dignified but unnoteworthy-looking gentlemen arrived at my office. The man I understood to be the father was approximately eighty, and his son seemed close to sixty. They spoke with heavy Lithuanian accents. Dressed in their ties and checked suits, they appeared elegant in a pre–World War II way. On the street, I might have mistaken them for jewelers or merchants from a diamond district. Both men were gentle and unassuming in their manner.

I had anticipated that my guests might approach me with skepticism and be on their guard. They were members of a secret society, after all! To my surprise, that was not the case at all. I found them to be congenial and seemingly at ease with me. At the time, if I had had to guess why, I probably would have said that after thoroughly vetting me, maybe they figured I may have something valuable to share and that at the very least, I wasn't a threat to them.

We all sat down on the couch in my office and started to talk. I was honored to be with them and ready to absorb anything they were willing to share. The father proudly explained that Freemasonry (also called "Masonry") is the world's first and largest fraternity, based on the belief that each man can make a difference in the world. To this day, the order is (almost) exclusively male, and its ostensible purpose is to make "better men out of good men."[21] He went on to explain that they believe there's more to life than pleasure or money, and that they strive to live with honor, integrity, and philanthropic values. Intrigued, I asked how the organization got started.

The son jumped in and said that Freemasonry goes back some seven hundred years, with its roots in the medieval fraternities of stoneworkers.[22] Masons were very prominent in early American life—revolutionaries Alexander Hamilton and Paul Revere were members, as were presidents George Washington and Andrew Jackson. In fact, at least fourteen American presidents, including Harry Truman and Gerald Ford, have been Masons,[23] which blew me away. Never having joined a fraternity in college myself, I was fascinated by the idea of these historical luminaries devoting themselves to a shared philosophy and a code of conduct so shrouded in mystery that most people didn't even know it existed. The time flew by as father and son answered my many questions, sometimes in great detail, other times more opaquely (they weren't sharing *everything*).

After a good hour, the father turned to me and said, "Brian, would you ever consider joining us, becoming a member of the Masons?" In that moment, the meeting, which had started as a curiosity conversation, turned into something quite different—a proposal. My eyes opened wide in surprise, as though I had just been given an unexpected compliment. I didn't have to say a word. The look in my eyes and a slight tilt of the head communicated my receptivity to the idea.

He continued, "Well, we've talked about it. And we feel you are an excellent candidate. We just have one question we would like to ask you."

"What's that?" I said. Although I was trying to play it cool, I was super excited. I couldn't believe that they wanted me to be a member of their secret society!

"We need to know if there is any way in which you would ever betray us."

I was a bit startled. It was a powerful question with historical resonance. There is a reason why the Freemasons' membership process includes something called "the third degree" (yes, that's where the phrase comes from).[24] The Masons are no strangers to treachery and have been the subject of their fair share of conspiracy theories. They have been persecuted under various Communist regimes and were directly targeted by the Nazis.[25] It's estimated that somewhere between 80,000 and 200,000 were killed in the Holocaust.[26]

I immediately recognized a shift in the tone of our conversation. Where before the exchange had been free-flowing and convivial, now it took on a gravity that required a more measured response. When the Masons asked if I would ever betray them, they were not asking lightly. Nor was this a mere formality. It was absolutely critical for them to know my answer, and my answer would have to be 100 percent sincere.

My mind was racing at lightning speed. I wondered whether I *could* betray them and what that would even look like. I was certain I would never overtly violate their trust, but the Masons have a very strict standard of conduct and an elite reputation to protect.[27] What if I messed up inadvertently? *It* is maybe *possible,* I thought, *that I could do something that they would* perceive *to be a violation of their code.* After all, I'm a pretty spontaneous guy who likes his humor and fair share of creature comforts.

As I considered the situation, I glanced at the two men. In their eyes I found trust and kindness. Getting to know them over the past hour, I felt that they were gentlemen of character. They had given me their full attention, looking at me intently throughout our conversation. They were also impeccable listeners, who expressed appreciation for the recurring themes of human courage and empowerment in my work. In short, they had treated me with the utmost respect. I wanted to reciprocate that and honor the connection we had made. Even though I was flattered and tempted by the invitation to join their very exclusive organization, I *knew* what I had to say. In my heart I knew that my interest in the group wasn't fully aligned with their greater purpose. Or *my* greater purpose.

"I'm sorry," I responded. "But I can't do it."

The father looked at me with surprise. He was clearly taken aback by my decision. The son looked at the father to gauge how he should react, and he followed suit. It wasn't exactly a comfortable moment for me, but I knew in my gut that it was the right one.

If you are sincere, actively listening, and present with the people you are face to face with, a pact forms. By inviting me into their secret brotherhood, the Masons elevated the level of the pact and changed the nature of the conversation—at least they did for me. I had come to the meeting with no agenda beyond learning more about them and their organization. The Masons, on the other hand, came to the meeting as people interested in connecting with power players across a variety of fields—politics, education, industry, technology, and the arts. For them, this was a chance to feel out and possibly recruit a new member.

If I hadn't been paying attention, I could easily have misunderstood the seriousness of their invitation and made a flip decision about something of great consequence. However, because I was attuned from the start, not only listening but also taking in nonverbal cues, I saw the situation for what it was and was able to adapt accordingly.

In hindsight, some of the questions the Masons posed might have clued me in earlier as to the direction in which things were headed. For example, I can see now that when they asked, "Brian, do you believe in God?," they were evaluating whether I fulfilled that requirement of their code. However, the important thing is that I got it right in the end. To this day, I don't know what might have happened if I had accepted the Masons' offer of membership (although I suspect they would have taken issue with my film *The Da Vinci Code*, given the conspiracy theories it revived). What I do know is that I have never regretted my decision to decline.

CHAPTER 11

Curiosity in the Kremlin

*"Anyone who has never made a mistake
has never tried anything new."*

—Albert Einstein

I've worked pretty hard to make connections, and to understand connection cues, but as far as I've come in interpreting
connections and staying alert to people's cues, I have also had
my own share of mishaps, which tells me I can always keep
learning. We all can spin stuff consciously or unconsciously
when we want something to happen, rationalizing away any
signals that might guide us to a conclusion we don't want to
hear. This happened to me a few years ago.

I grew up during the Cold War. As a kid, I picked up that
Russians were the enemy and stood for all that was anti-
thetical to the core democratic values of America. I feared
that they would emerge from behind the "Iron Curtain" and
destroy our way of life. Because of the way that the Soviet
Union was structured and their lack of independent media,
there wasn't a whole lot that I actually knew about the USSR
outside of what I saw in movies. But as a young boy coming
of age in the late fifties and early sixties, I couldn't imagine

a place less hospitable to visit. Going to the Soviet Union seemed just about as unlikely as—in fact, more so than—visiting the moon.

Maybe I'm just attracted, as most people are, to things that are forbidden and dangerous, but as I grew older, I became more curious about visiting the USSR. It was only recently, however, that I got my chance.

Ever since Vladimir Putin first became president of Russia, I've wanted to meet him for a curiosity conversation. Sure, he's one of the most feared leaders in the world. But as a person of tremendous power and influence (maybe that's putting it a bit mildly), an emblem of both contemporary Russia and the Cold War, and a former KGB officer, Putin intrigues me. Which isn't to say that I agree with his methods or tactics, or with any of his beliefs. I often have conversations—by design—with people whose views and values don't always align with my own. I've met with members of cartels and the Yakuza (a transnational, organized crime syndicate originating in Japan); I've met with Fidel Castro and also Daryl Gates, the controversial former chief of the Los Angeles Police Department during the LA riots. Not everyone I meet is Jonas Salk. My goal is to widen my perspective, to enlarge the way I see the world, even if doing so is uncomfortable.

But how does one engineer a meeting with the likes of Vladimir Putin? You can't just pick up the phone and start asking around for an invitation. It didn't seem realistic to meet him, so I never really pursued it. Though whenever I was asked who I wanted to meet most for a curiosity conversation, I would say Putin. Apparently, my interest got some word of mouth.

A few years ago, I had a young employee named Scott, a sharp guy whose father, Steve, was involved in the world of bonding films. Bonding a movie simply ensures that a movie gets finished; it's a type of insurance called a completion guarantor. His company bonded movies everywhere you can imagine—and so they had an extensive network reaching all over the globe. Scott's father had been doing it for decades. Based on our conversations while working together, Scott knew I wanted to meet Putin, and months after he'd moved on from the job at Imagine, he called me.

"Putin's team reached out to my father's business associates," he said. "Putin is interested in meeting you. He'd be willing to have a conversation." This sounded fishy. It seemed highly improbable that the Russian president would be proactively reaching out to have a conversation with me.

"Really?" Scott had always wanted to please me, I thought to myself skeptically. But the part of me that was excited by this turn of events rationalized it; I wasn't his boss anymore, so he didn't have any real incentive to butter me up. I asked, "How did this happen? How'd you hear about it? Tell me every single detail."

"My father told me," he said. "He'd mentioned to his business associate who happens to be a Russian oligarch that you wanted to meet Putin, and word came back down the chain that Putin, in fact, wants to meet you."

Hmm.

This sounded, in essence, like a game of telephone; who knew what Putin had heard—if he'd heard anything—let alone what he'd said? Things get misinterpreted that way in a grade-school classroom. Imagine how much distortion could occur between Los Angeles and Moscow. Still, I decided to check it out—to see, at least, if the invitation had any merit.

I happened to have another friend—a producer—whose family was similarly connected with some influential Russians. He is a smart, thorough, reliable guy, who is pretty savvy about these things. I called and asked him to check it out for me. Soon enough, he called me back.

"It's true," he said. "It's real."

"Well, what do you mean 'real'?" I asked.

"I mean I checked it out. I saw the emails and vetted the people involved." Normally, I'm quick to question quick-fire replies to complicated questions. This time, however, I suppressed that instinct and kept the hope of the invitation alive.

"Well, I'd like to see the emails and hear more about what you found out," I said.

I wondered if the emails would be genuine, and sure enough, they appeared to be. Another Russian friend of mine validated that these were indeed actual government addresses and that the emails contained a confirmed invitation to meet. *Okay*, I thought, *I'm finally going to Russia.*

"I'd like to go with you," Scott said. Given that he was the one who brought me the opportunity, I said okay. The Russians had agreed to pay for everything and for anyone I wanted to bring to Moscow, so it wasn't any skin off my back to bring him along. It was now a small group of people (Scott and Steve) who'd be traveling with me. Veronica was coming too.

Just a couple of weeks after this, we found ourselves in the Lufthansa First Class lounge at LAX. There was a tall, really intense Russian guy there to meet us—I never did get his name. He had the blackest hair I'd ever seen. It looked dyed, like it had been dipped in ink. There was another guy, also hulking, named Huntington, who was American. These two were well-known to have financed movies in America, and were associated with Steve in some way. But I didn't understand why they were traveling with us. What I did notice was that the black-haired Russian, since the moment he met us in the lounge, was perspiring. Heavily. He had beads of perspiration on his upper lip, which seemed odd to me for a guy who had been sitting still for the last half hour. Normally, the unexplained sweating would have been a yellow flag for me when engaging with someone on something of importance—like accompanying me on a trip to Russia! It was yet another observation that added to the feeling of uncertainty, this sense that I might be getting into something more than I'd bargained for. But I turned a blind eye to it.

The flight was easy and seamless. We touched down in Moscow and were whisked past customs—we barely had to flash our passports—and we were zipped away in Rolls-Royces. They took us to the Ararat Park Hyatt (they'd originally said they were going to put us up in The Ritz-Carlton; I'm not particularly paranoid, but this, too, was something I noticed), and then took us through our itinerary. That night, a Sunday, we were going to be taken to some sort of penthouse, an elegant Russian restaurant, for caviar and champagne. The next day, at noon, according to Steve, who had been coordinating with our local hosts, we were supposed to meet with Putin's press secretary, Dmitry Peskov. On Tuesday afternoon at three, we were set to meet Putin himself.

It all sounded fine. Only, I still didn't know why, exactly, Putin would invite me to meet with him. Then again, there has not been one leader or head of state who has said no to meeting me for a curiosity conversation. I told myself it was possible that he heard about these conversations with world leaders and wanted to have one as well.

We had our caviar and champagne. Slightly less caviar, somehow, than I'd expected. (I don't know why this surprised me. I think I was just attuned to even the smallest of discrepancies, the ever so slight differences between what was promised—our interpreters had made it sound, somehow, like there'd be mountains of the stuff—and what appeared.) Even if it was odd for them to try and entice me with caviar when they had already gotten me to make the trip, I told myself to forget it. We were now in Moscow and I was getting closer to the big meeting.

On Monday morning we woke up and were greeted at the hotel by another group of Russians. One of them, very sleek and muscular, was dressed from head to toe in black: leather pants, leather jacket, and motorcycle boots. He looked a bit like Jean Reno in *Léon: The Professional*: sullen and intense.

"This is Sergey. Brian, say hello."

I did. He didn't say a word, just looked me up and down very deliberately and shook my hand. Then he turned around and left just like that.

"Who was that?" I asked Scott's father.

"That is Putin's very good friend."

"His 'good friend'?"

"He teaches Putin martial arts. He just needed to look at you."

Well, that was unusual, I thought to myself. Then again, I did make an entire television series called *Lie to Me* about a world-famous physiognomist who studies faces to determine whether someone is telling the truth or not. So who was I to judge? And of course it made sense that someone like Putin would want to have me checked out by someone he trusted.

Off we went to meet with Peskov at the Kremlin, which wasn't very far from the hotel. Once there, we were told that only a few of us were going to be allowed into the meeting. The other Russians who had showed up that morning left. Fair enough. This wasn't the most inclusive environment, and I had no idea who those guys were anyway. Scott, his father, the two guys who'd met us at LAX—Huntington and the sweating Russian—and I would be allowed into the meeting with Peskov.

To say that the Kremlin is a pretty tense place would be an understatement (after all, the etymology of the word "kremlin" shows that it does mean fortress). If you've been on a tour of the White House, you know that it's ceremonious, a place that inspires a certain respectful restraint—but it isn't tense. Not the way the Kremlin felt, anyway. The feeling was like being planted in a seventies spy movie, reminiscent of *Three Days of the Condor* or such.

As we were led down a long hallway, we passed steely face after steely face. A nondescript assistant with yet another steely face ushered us into a rather small, stark waiting room. With just a small table in the corner and not enough chairs, some of us sat and some of us stood and waited. Peskov was late. Our restlessness spiked. No one was speaking, just nervously looking around at each other, pretending this was normal. It was so silent, I thought I could hear the ticking of my watch. Huntington and the Russian seemed particularly nervous as we waited. Exactly ten minutes later, we were led into Peskov's office. The assistant gestured for us to sit around a conference table, leaving the head seat open for her boss.

I tried to keep things in perspective. A friend of mine who'd met him had once described Peskov in terms that seemed not so worrisome. "I like him a lot. He's a good guy," he had said. I sat there and willed myself to believe that Putin's press secretary might be even remotely approachable! Finally, he came in. He was . . . not exactly what I'd call welcoming.

"Mr. Peskov," I said, trying, as I normally do at meetings, to make some inroads and create a more relaxed and comfortable atmosphere. "My good friend"—I named him—"wanted me to say hello."

Peskov looked at me blankly and nodded. Not even a hint of emotion. He sat with his hands clasped, folded in front of him. He was exactly as you'd expect Vladimir Putin's right hand to be: impatient, chilly. Eventually, he cut to the chase.

"What is it that you want?" His stern voice cut through the tension-thick air like a knife.

"I don't really 'want' anything," I said. "I thought this was set up by you."

I didn't go any further. I'd let the other people in the room, the ones who'd actually helped organize this meeting, do the talking. Maybe they could explain why we were here and why, shockingly, it seemed as if Peskov had no idea what that reason was.

"We are here because Brian loves our country," said the sweaty Russian, the tall man with the perspiring upper lip and the inky hair. "He would like to do a film about our president. He made *A Beautiful Mind*, which celebrated the achievements of the mathematician John Nash, and he would like to do a similar thing for our country. He feels as if for twenty years people in the West have been misled about what happens in Russia, which he loves. He also feels like the American government is a puppet regime."

I stared at him. Not a single word of this was true (except for the part about *A Beautiful Mind*. I had indeed produced that movie, but every other word was a flaming falsehood). Not only was it untrue, but I'd been explicit about my intentions for the trip with everyone involved from the very beginning.

No one else in the room seemed to be acknowledging what was happening. I looked over at my traveling companions, but they seemed willing to go along with the idea that this was why I'd come. I turned to Peskov determined to inject the truth into this meeting.

"I'm sorry," I said in a firm tone. I reached out and grabbed the sweaty Russian's wrist, but I kept my eyes focused on Peskov. "That is absolutely not true. I have no intention of ever making a movie about President Putin, or about Russia. I don't make movies about contemporary politics to begin with. I don't even know this man who's speaking!"

As Peskov looked back at me, I could finally see that he knew the Russian guy was trying to BS him and that I was telling the truth. It was clear enough that the meeting had been set under false pretenses.

"I'm sorry," I said again. "I came here simply to meet the president and have a conversation without an agenda in mind, just like I've done with Barack Obama, Ronald Reagan, Fidel Castro, and Margaret Thatcher."

He shook his head. Not a chance that was happening. No way.

"Look," I continued. "It's probably best to end this here. I don't think it makes sense to meet with President Putin."

"Correct," he said. "That is absolutely correct."

As we brought things to a close, what astounded me—flabbergasted me, really—was the way that everyone else in the room seemed to be in some alternate reality where the meeting had been a smashing success. "What a great meeting!" they told each other. One of them—the guy with the sweaty lip—piped up. "Brian, why don't we take a photograph of you two together?"

No way, I thought. All I wanted was to get out of there. I glanced at Peskov. He wasn't too keen on the picture idea either.

"No photographs," he said sternly.

We shook hands. He mentioned that if I ever did want to make a movie, that I should reach out to him.

That meeting was destined to disappoint. Nothing was going to allow Peskov and I to get what we both wanted. I wanted a curiosity conversation with the Russian president. The press secretary, to do his job (which, presumably, includes shielding the Russian president from ambiguous meetings like the one I was proposing). Our desires were completely incompatible, mutually exclusive, really, and no amount of eye contact or persuasion was going to change that.

The large majority of the time, the attempt to connect results in something positive. But not every connection works out the way we hope. When we are paying attention, we can see the signs of these failed connections early on and prevent messes like the one I walked into in Russia. The thing is, when we really, really want something to happen, we often rationalize and tell ourselves stories to justify anything that doesn't align with our desired narrative. Tracing back every step (which Veronica and I did in excruciating detail on the long flight home), I realize that I did exactly that. But I had wanted so badly to sit down with Putin for a curiosity conversation that I ignored my "informed" intuition.

Does this experience discourage me from pursuing intimidating or challenging connections? Not at all. Next time though, I won't ignore it when the caviar seems a little short.

CHAPTER 12

What Words Can't Say

*"There is a language that is beyond words. If I can
learn to decipher that language without words,
I will be able to decipher the world."*

—Paulo Coelho

Years ago, I had flown into Hong Kong for business and found
myself wide awake in the middle of the night. Terrible jet
lag was part of it. But I was also having a hard time turning
off my mind. This was in 1989, when Ron and I were in the
midst of taking our company, Imagine Entertainment, public. There's always anxiety involved in taking your business
public, and my brain was busy trying to process everything
we still needed to do. One of my concerns was the need for
a larger office space back in Los Angeles. Over the course of
two years, we'd gone from being a company of fifteen people
to having nine times as many (accountants, production executives, a COO, a CFO, a head of business affairs). Our current office could barely contain us, and I knew the situation
would only be getting worse.

Unable to sleep, I got out of bed and stared out my hotel
room window. Somewhere out there, shrouded in a dense

cloud of fog, was Victoria Harbour. As I looked, a form started to emerge—an imposing skyscraper. At that hour, and under those conditions, both the base and top of the building were obscured, but the center of it rose, gleaming, through the mist. Even then, it was a hypnotic, powerful sight. In the morning, after I'd managed a few hours of sleep and the fog had cleared, I took another look. The building was just as stunning as I'd thought. In the clear light of day, I recognized the distinct style of the architect I. M. Pei at work. I also noted how the building completely dominated the skyline.

Later, down in the lobby, I asked the hotel manager about it.

"That's the Bank of China Tower," he told me. Today, of course, the building is internationally famous, but at the time it was only recently constructed and not even occupied yet. "Everyone in Hong Kong is very upset about it. There's been an enormous uproar among the owners and proprietors of the neighboring buildings, particularly among the feng shui experts."

"Feng shui" was not a widely known term in the U.S. back then and I had no clue what the manager was talking about.

"What are those?" I asked. "The feng shui experts?"

He explained to me that these were consultants hired routinely by businesses to identify the most auspicious architectural and interior design arrangements: where to place doors, windows, and furniture to harmonize, which things signify trust and the influx of money, and so on. I don't know that I am a superstitious person, but I was fascinated by the concept. Particularly given my preoccupation with our hunt for office space.

I spent the next few days of my trip asking around about feng shui consultants—who were the best and most highly regarded in Hong Kong? It became a matter of urgent curiosity for me that went beyond its relevance to my business. I was dying to know more about this unfamiliar idea.

Eventually I found my way to the people I'd been looking for—two brothers renowned and highly sought after for their expertise in feng shui. Gaining access to them, especially as a Westerner, was difficult and involved a fair amount of ceremony. I was growing increasingly worried that there would be no meeting with the consultants. But then, on the very last day of my trip, it happened.

The two brothers met me in my hotel room. I presented them with an envelope containing a generous donation; this was customary, and they didn't look inside. As I do with any other curiosity conversation, I had prepared as best I could for the meeting. However, I don't speak any Cantonese and, though it was lucky for me they spoke any English, their command of the language wasn't great. I had to rely on my eyes to do a good deal of the communication and paid very close attention to theirs as well. I leaned in and watched them very, very closely as we spoke. To the best of my ability, I asked them about what they did and how they did it. Did their expertise extend beyond the placement of furniture, doors, and windows? How did they know what to do? I still hold the memory of one of the brothers remarking, in his halting but strangely idiomatic English, that they proceeded by virtue of feeling themselves "connected to the source."

We struggled through most of the conversation. Then, just before the meeting concluded, one of them leaned over and took me by the wrists. He studied my hands for a moment, and my arms. Then the other brother did the same.

"Do you have a person in your life," the first brother asked, "with the initials Q. N.?"

I thought for a moment. It was an uncommon set of initials, but I ran a fairly large company and had a lot of other people in my life too. I watched him almost as if I were going to see the image of a particular person reflected in his eyes.

"I'm not sure, but I might," I said. "Yes."

"Be careful," he said. "This person, Q. N., is going to be very dangerous to you in your life."

I instantly believed him. I could feel the credibility of the information coming to me through his eyes.

I thanked them and set off for the airport. All the way there and for the entire flight home, I thought about Q. N. and the look in the brothers' eyes, which flashed with warning and intention.

Back in LA, the logistical headaches awaited. It was great that we'd raised a fair share of capital, but our company still didn't have its offices.

I was thrilled then, when, upon my return, Robin Barris, one of our senior executives, pulled me aside. "We found something. Quinn," she said, naming one of the consultants we'd hired to help with the office search, "found a great spot for us to move into. It's a ten-year lease on a space in Bel Air."

"Bel Air?" It seemed pretty out of the way and largely residential. Most entertainment offices in Los Angeles tend to cluster in a corridor around Wilshire Boulevard in Beverly Hills or Santa Monica.

"How'd he find it?"

Robin explained that Quinn (his name, of course, stood out immediately; his last name, indeed, began with an *N* as well) had heard about the building through a relative.

"Would you look into it a little deeper?" I asked Robin. "I know you say it's a great space, and ten years is a reasonable term for the lease and all that, but it's a lot of money to pay into a space we don't own. Who owns that building?"

I might have known before she did. The people who were to stand on the receiving end of our lease payments were none other than Quinn himself, along with a college friend of his who had become a realtor. Turns out had we locked ourselves into ten years of payments, at the end of the term *they* would have owned the building. We narrowly avoided signing the papers.

"Get rid of Quinn," I told her. "Don't offer any explanation—just let him go."

She did. He left without any argument. He knew he had been found out.

A story like this always feels like it contains shades of coincidence. The brothers' warning to me was not specific, and there are other people with the initials Q. N. in the world. So I'm not going to argue that there was some divine or mystical force at work during that meeting in Hong Kong. But I do believe that information is transmitted—in fact, I *know* that information is transmitted—in many, many ways that transcend the verbal.

That's what the whole discipline of feng shui is about, after all, and that's what my conversation with the two men—which was barely a conversation at all in the conventional sense—was about too.

We spoke with our words but also, more important, with our attention and our intention. Who knows what was "said" in that respect? I believe they understood me better than many people whose English is flawless and with whom I've exchanged words by the bucketful.

I travel quite a bit for both work and pleasure. As was the case in Hong Kong, I rarely know the native language of the places I visit. I mean that both in terms of spoken language and in terms of nonverbal language. On a trip to Israel, for example, I noticed that when our Israeli guide ran into a friend, he slapped each side of the man's face with strong hands. As the two smiled and seemed to enjoy a loud and lively conversation, he shook his friend's cheeks up and down. I noted to

Veronica—more than once—that I would have felt assaulted had a friend done that to me.

Knowing that different cultures have different ways of using eye contact and body language to communicate, I strive to be extremely attentive and sensitive to this information when I am in another country. I have to be if I want to form strong, meaningful connections with the people I meet there—and forming those kinds of relationships is to me what traveling is all about.

A few years ago, Veronica and I decided to go to Burma. For years my friend Tom Freston, one of the founders of MTV and former CEO of Viacom, had been telling me I needed to go, but Tom is something of an adventurous traveler. He has frequently invited me to join him in places like Baghdad or Kabul, places that while surely fascinating are not necessarily where I would choose to go on vacation! Still, Tom always has his finger on the pulse when it comes to those rare, off-the-beaten-path gems. And Burma lingered in my mind.

I was working on the movie *Get On Up* with Mick Jagger, who was also a producer, and we spent quite a bit of downtime together on the set in Natchez, Mississippi. One day I asked him where he liked to go most on vacation. After all, Mick Jagger knows a thing or two about how to live. Without hesitation he said, "Inle Lake, in Myanmar. Burma." Well. Now two experienced travelers with impeccable taste were telling me this was the place to go. I figured I *had* to check it out. Veronica, herself an adventurer (she once climbed

Mount Kilimanjaro on a whim and had been diving in the Philippines without formal training), loved the idea. She booked the trip the next day, planning it all out with a local travel agent who knew the region extremely well and could ensure an authentic experience. That's always super important to us when we travel.

When we touched down in Yangon (formerly Rangoon), we were met by our guide, a wonderful and wise Burmese woman in her fifties named Kiki. Only recently open to tourism, Myanmar is not an easy place to visit. The country has a volatile political history full of horrid human rights abuses, military regimes, and voter suppression. Kiki, we later learned, had grown up amid this turbulence and terror. Her own father had been thrown in jail for years. Yet she still saw beauty in this country that she loved and, as a guide, she wanted visitors to experience that side of her homeland as well.

We embarked on a nine-day journey with Kiki, culminating in a visit to Inle Lake, our long-awaited destination. One of the most stunning lakes in the world, it's situated in a valley between two mountain ranges. This raw and expansive body of water seemed to reflect the surrounding beauty like glass. Dotted with active villages on stilts and illuminated by Buddhist temples rising from the water, the place was extraordinary. Told that the best way to experience the lake would be by canoe, we chose to travel in a slender, long-tail wooden version used by the locals.

During our three days on the lake, we watched as farmers with water buffalo tilled the rice paddies and residents of tilt villages went about their daily chores. Locals in weathered boats drifted by us, selling hand-carved Buddha statues, tourist knickknacks, and oranges grown in nearby floating gardens. Periodically, we would stop to explore a village, where we would visit a chaotic farmers' market or learn a cottage industry. Young girls and old women hand-rolled cheroots (thin cigars) in the lakeside stalls and grandmothers sold noodles. Small children delighted in a game of sticks.

A woman welcomed us into her family's umbrella-making workshop. She walked us through the intricate and time-consuming process of crafting each piece by hand. We watched closely as her younger daughter, who couldn't have been more than ten years old, made paper pulp from a mulberry tree, while her father cranked a foot-powered lathe to shape the wooden handles. The little girl put flower petals in my hands and guided them through a pool of water to create a design on the wet paper pulp. Different parts of the final product were produced by various family members and assembled in the end to create the most beautiful umbrellas in a rainbow of vibrant colors, patterns, and sizes. I was moved, knowing that we were witnessing cultural traditions and practices that had been handed down from generation to generation.

On our final night at Inle Lake, Veronica and I went out on the canoe at sunset to experience the silence and emptiness of this magical place. We lay back and took in the infinite red and gold layers settling over the water. I was feeling emotional thinking about what we had experienced here. Coming from the world of Hollywood where people tend to have complex and, at times, questionable motivations, I was delighted by the transparency and realness of our interactions with the Burmese people.

I remembered one morning when we had stopped to talk with an elderly woman in one of the villages. She had been checking us out with a friendly but curious gaze. With the help of Kiki's translation and some deliberate nonverbal signals, we quickly understood that they rarely saw tourists here; the woman was enthralled by Veronica's blond hair. Although we were strangers to her, the woman invited us into her home to share in a traditional breakfast of *mohinga*. The fish-based broth with rice noodles (and lots of condiments on the side!) was absolutely delicious, made all the better by the warmth of our host. There were so many stories of connections like this one. Among all of the connections we made, however, none was as special as the one we formed with Kiki.

For more than a week, Kiki had traveled the country with us, by boat, plane, train, and foot. She had been with us when we visited the Buddhist monasteries in the north, an orphanage deep in the countryside, and a remote village where they still draw water from the town well. She facilitated authentic exchanges with locals and shared her own unique perspectives with us.

The Burmese government is aggressively concerned with how their country is presented to outsiders. So becoming a guide is no easy feat. Kiki had to complete a tremendous amount of work and pass a number of difficult tests to do her job. Not unsurprisingly, she was careful in her historical narration. But when she shared personal stories describing her family and their deep connection to the land, Kiki would truly come alive. Through Kiki's emotional lens, we were able to experience the country in a way we will never forget.

With the trip coming to an end, it was time for us to say good-bye to our beloved guide and new friend. Standing on the tarmac, I moved to give Kiki a hug. It was completely instinctual, the kind of affectionate gesture that is the norm for Americans. To my surprise, she stepped away. Still, she kept her eyes trained on my own.

I backed up out of respect. "I'm sorry," I started to say, but she stopped me with her open and understanding gaze. "I *know*," she said, indicating that it was okay. "I know."

In that moment, I understood: She wasn't refusing the affection, just the embrace. Kiki explained that people in her culture don't hug. Instead, during moments of greeting and parting, moments of emotional connection, they look one another in the eyes, because the eyes, Kiki told us, "are the window to the soul." "We see everything we need to know," she said, "by looking in each other's eyes. Hugging seems almost dishonest."

(In fact, there's some science behind the idea that the

eyes reveal the depth and authenticity of affection. It was a French physician named Guillaume Duchenne who discovered that the crow's-feet that accompany a genuine smile are controlled by muscles that cannot be moved voluntarily. Only a genuine smile will reveal those creases around the corners of the eyes.)

The exchange with Kiki on the tarmac was poignant not only because it signified the end of an unexpectedly meaningful vacation, but also because it introduced me to a new and profound way of connecting to another human. As soon as Veronica and I settled in on the plane, we looked at each other, tears in our eyes, and vowed to bring our family back to Burma.

So we did. The very next Christmas, we journeyed back to Inle Lake with our kids. Once again, we experienced the country in a way that was deep and beautiful, only now it was amplified by the fact that we were seeing it through the eyes of our children. This time departing, we all knew. We didn't need to say it. We wouldn't give a hug. We knew to honor the connection with our local hosts by offering gratitude with our eyes, the windows to our souls.

CHAPTER 13

Where Life Begins

*"Life will only change when you become
more committed to your dreams than
to your comfort zone."*

—Billy Cox

My wife and I have two teenagers at home and have come to realize that eating together is one of the only times that we have a chance for real conversations with them. To keep this time sacred, she and I decided we needed a way to create boundaries with our devices during meals, so all of us put our cell phones in a basket before we eat. It's better than simply setting our screens down, because the mere presence of a phone next to a person is distracting in and of itself.[28] This practice has freed us to have interesting and enlightening conversations with the kids that are able to stretch to more than just one-syllable answers! It also inspired one of our favorite family traditions.

In an effort to celebrate birthdays in a less materialistic way that would make each person feel valued by other family members, we came up with an activity. We go around the table and everyone has to give a toast while looking the person with the birthday in the eye. If the person is at the far end of the table from you, or you can't face them directly, you have to get up so that you can. As you can imagine, the kids hated it in the early days. Patrick and Thomas would shrink down in their chairs to avoid having to go next. But then little by little they became really good at it. These days, they raise their hands to go first!

We taught the kids that the easiest toast or speech is the one that is not made up of a bunch of generic "nice" adjectives, but rather one that comes straight from the heart. We encouraged them to share a story about the person, a memory that would make them feel good. ("Yeah! I almost died when Riley jumped up and danced with the locals!" or "Remember when we were camping and Sage got a fever? Patrick wouldn't let go of her hand all night!") They loved seeing how their toasts could make the family laugh and cry and earn them shout-outs. This ritual has led to some of our most memorable moments as a family. Not to mention, the kids have gotten pretty darn good at public speaking!

When we were on a boat for a family vacation a couple of summers ago, it happened to fall over Father's Day, so the kids prepared toasts for me. Veronica likes to come up with themes and asked them to focus on something I taught them that still sticks with them today. My daughter, Sage, now thirty-one years old, recalled a time when I spoke to her about the importance of disrupting her comfort zone. She said this was one of the things that made her brave enough

to abandon her four-year pursuit of a career in photography and instead pursue her dream of becoming a psychotherapist (which she is today); it brought me to tears. It made me feel amazing to know that I have empowered my kids to step outside their comfort zones, because I truly believe that is where the most memorable moments of our lives can happen.

Several years ago, I got a call from my good friend Tom Freston, the friend I mentioned earlier who had recommended we visit Myanmar. Tom invited me on a last-minute guys trip to Senegal with a group that included the singer Dave Matthews, and vocalist and guitarist Trey Anastasio from the band Phish. The motivation for the trip was twofold: a reunion concert for Orchestra Baobab, masters of African/Afro-Cuban music that dominated Senegal's music scene in the seventies, and a private concert with Baaba Maal, a remarkable musician and contemporary globetrotter who had become an African hero in the eighties when his sound brought him to an international audience.

It was sure to be a thrilling adventure. But I wasn't sure. If I went, I would have to clear my entire schedule that week without much notice. It would mean a full day of travel to the other side of the world. And once there, I'd be spending 24/7 with a group of guys who, other than Tom, I had never met before. There were a lot of unknowns and a lot of inconveniences to consider. I could have easily said no with good reason. But I didn't. I said yes. I was curious about the country, the culture, the people, the guys who were going, and

these talented musicians who had created so much attention. I'd be stepping outside my comfort zone, but I thought it would be worth it.

As soon as we landed down in Dakar, we quickly dropped our bags at the hotel and headed out into the city. We were all anxious and excited to get a feel for this exotic and alluring place. First stop was Dakar's largest market, Sandaga. Lively and buzzy, it was packed with stalls hawking everything you could possibly imagine, from African masks and carvings to local fabrics and exotic fruits. The influence of Senegal's French colonizers also came through. Some of it was touristy for sure, but we liked mingling with the local Senegalese as they shopped for the day's requirements. We watched as suit-clad businessmen knelt down in the middle of the street for prayer, and talked to a woman who convinced us to try a popular street food called *accra*. The crispy black-eyed-bean fritters served with a tomato-and-onion-based hot sauce called *kaani* reminded me of Southern hush puppies. Delicious!

The next morning we ventured out of the city to see Lake Retba, otherwise called Lac Rose, a body of water nestled between white sand dunes and the Atlantic Ocean. It was a stunning and memorable visual: a brilliant shade of strawberry pink that gets its color from algae. As we got out of the truck, dozens of village children ran up to us and grabbed our hands. They led us down the beach as their fathers worked to harvest salt from the lake with spades and sticks, and their mothers waited ashore to help haul the filled buckets from

the boat to the land. This basic industry would create income for families from surrounding countries such as Mali, Ivory Coast, and Guinea.[29] That afternoon, we traveled to Gorée Island, a UNESCO World Heritage site that was once the largest slave-trading center on the African coast. G. W. Bush, Clinton, and Obama have made the pilgrimage here, as has Nelson Mandela. It was a somber reminder of the deep and complex history of where we were.

That evening would be the first of two of the most captivating musical experiences I've ever had in my life. Baaba Maal was performing for the Senegalese aristocracy, and we were lucky enough to be his guests. Sitting on the floor with about seventy-five others, we watched as three priestess singers in long, flowing, colorful Senegalese dresses appeared. Their nearly imperceptible, slow-motion moves, which gradually picked up speed throughout the performance, were almost hypnotic. Just then, Baaba Maal himself, wearing a magnificent red robe, arrived with dramatic flair. Instead of a big first number, he broke into a delicate and soulful piece, surprising us with bursts of sudden power. He's a breathtaking performer, and brought the crowd to a point of mania, again and again. The three-hour experience built to a high-energy closing act that left me in a state of complete euphoria.

As the concert finished in the wee hours, we headed outside to feast on a freshly slaughtered goat, a cultural tradition they were proud for us to partake in. There, I met Baaba, and he was as charismatic and exuberant as one might expect after seeing him perform. At the same time, he was serene and thoughtful as he talked about where he came from: He grew up by a river in a rural village named Djoum, as part of the Fulani, a seminomadic people.[30] Having spent a lifetime on the road as a musician, he talked about the feeling of coming back home and how there's nothing quite like it. He said, "You realize you're still you," but with new connections and experiences that become a part of you. I could certainly relate to that.

The next evening we headed over to the reunion of the famed Orchestra Baobab. The concert was at a local venue on the outskirts of Dakar, over an hour's drive from our hotel. It was so dark, it felt like the middle of the night as we made our way there. By the time we arrived, the place was hot and crowded, everyone standing body to body. I waded through the audience toward the stage to get a closer look at who was behind this incredible sound, a fusion of Afro-Cuban rhythms and African traditional music that one might mistaken for the sounds of the Buena Vista Social Club. As the incredible vocals, drums, congas, and bass guitar of the band played at near-deafening volume, every single person swayed in unison. I was thoroughly immersed in the moment, not caring about anything other than the beat of the music pulsing through my body. It was surreal to feel so connected to a crowd of strangers in a place so foreign. Yet somehow we all understood the universal emotion that comes from experiencing music together.

Disrupting your comfort zone can lead to the most unexpectedly beautiful connections in our lives. In fact, what I've discovered over the years is that if I'm not taking a chance on connecting, then I'm missing possibilities that could have enormous internal, and external, rewards. If I'm *not* stepping outside my comfort zone—as often as possible—then I'm holding myself back from opportunities to learn, grow, and see the world differently through the eyes of others. Stepping outside your comfort zone means taking a risk. And sometimes, for whatever reason, the risk won't pay off. But in my experience, more often than not, it does. Being willing to disrupt your comfort zone, I've found, is where life really begins.

CHAPTER 14

Venturing into New Worlds

"The Sanskrit word namaste means 'the spirit in me honors the spirit in you.' Whenever you first make eye contact with another person, say 'Namaste' silently to yourself. This is a way of acknowledging that the being there is the same as the being here."

—Deepak Chopra

Growing up in the flats of Sherman Oaks (known as "the Valley"), my world was very small. I rarely ventured outside the three-mile radius that existed between my house and school, the grocery store, and my aunt Helen and uncle Bernie's house. My experience of the world was further restricted by my dyslexia. Where other people find ways to broaden their horizons and expand their views through books, that was not an option for me. With time, however, I discovered that there was a simple and accessible way to expand my borders and live a larger life—meeting people.

We are all trapped in our own patterns of thinking, being, and seeing. In fact, most of us get so used to seeing the world *our* way that we come to think that the world *is* that way. It's totally refreshing to be reminded, over and over, how different the world looks to other people. That's why I am constantly on the lookout for opportunities to connect with people whose experiences, views, and lifestyles are different from my own. Sometimes, this takes the form of arranged curiosity conversations with specific individuals.[31] But a lot of times, I simply start up exchanges with random strangers—a skateboarder, a bartender, a street artist, an astrologist—who for some reason catch my attention. Whoever they are and however it happens, every time I engage someone new, I have the chance to see the world through their eyes. My life is richer and I am a more empathetic, more compassionate and wiser person for it. Here are a few stories that have stuck with me.

Over the holidays one year, Veronica and I decided to visit Buenos Aires for the first time. On our last evening there, we had dinner at a modern yet intimate Argentine-Jewish restaurant called Fayer that a friend had recommended. We were early and the place was only about half-full. Sitting side by side on a banquette, we settled in with a bottle of wine and some warm pretzel bread. A magnetic waiter caught our attention. Despite his youthful looks, he could easily have been mistaken for a seasoned maitre d' who charmed every table with an authentic charisma. We noticed the exceeding care he took with the other diners and when he came around to take our order, were impressed by the way he answered our questions with meticulous detail and expert understanding.

We expressed our admiration and in doing so, opened up a conversation. We learned the waiter's name—Eduardo—and found out that only four years before he had been walking door to door looking for a job in a new city and a new country. Although he had no experience, this restaurant decided to give him a shot. He had been working there ever since.

As we chatted further, Eduardo shared that at age eighteen he made the difficult decision to leave his home in Venezuela. The country was in the midst of an economic crisis with high levels of violence and severe food shortages, so Eduardo believed he had to leave to create opportunity for himself.[32] I asked him what made him think that he would be able to find a job in a foreign country where he didn't know a soul. Eduardo explained that his ability to speak English gave him a leg up in a city popular with English-speaking tourists. How did he learn, I wanted to know. Before leaving home, he told us, he gave himself a crash course playing English-language video games.

As the evening went on, we shared anecdotes back and forth, and with every dish or drink he delivered, Eduardo revealed more personal details of his life. For example, he told us that he could barely stand being apart from his girlfriend, whom he was planning to bring over from Caracas and marry as soon as he saved enough money. He showed us photos of the two together, and talked about marrying her someday. We knew this guy could do anything he set his mind on. Our connection with Eduardo transformed a nice enough dinner into one we'll never forget.

————

At least once or twice a week, I would have lunch outside at Bouchon in Beverly Hills, only a few minutes' walk from my office. One day I was sitting alone on a conference call, talking and looking across the restaurant's terrace, which was largely empty as it was already late in the afternoon. I scanned the tables and my eyes fell on a man who was sitting at the far end of the patio. I noticed he was glancing back at me.

What had caught my eye was not the man's standard-issue black turtleneck and slacks, but his unbounded energy. As he carried on a conversation with another man seated beside him, his face exuded enthusiasm and his eyes blazed with life. There was such an intensity about him that looking at him was almost involuntary. I didn't even realize I was doing it at first.

It took me a minute or two to notice that beside the man was a chair of some sort. Not a wheelchair, exactly—not in the same way I was used to—but a sturdy, well-built wooden conveyance, practically like a *throne*, only with wheels. I also observed that the man's companion kept handing things to him. It occurred to me then that he must be the man's assistant.

As I was wrapping up my phone call, the assistant stood up and *lifted* the man from where he was sitting, into the sturdy wooden chair. Suddenly I understood: This man who positively dominated the entire patio with his presence, who seemed so animated was, in fact, immobile from the neck down.

In one sense, this was a thorny and rather complicated moment. Aren't we all taught to avert our eyes from others' conspicuous differences, to look away out of a sense of modesty or a fear of offending or embarrassing someone? Once I became aware of the man's state, that's exactly what I did. I looked down at my lap, breaking the connection that had formed when our eyes first met. But a moment later, I found myself looking straight at him again. I couldn't help myself. I was just so curious as to who this person was and what he was all about.

I stood up, crossed the terrace, and approached him. He greeted me with a gentle look. He seemed surprised that I'd come over, but not unhappy.

"Hi," I said. "Would you mind if I sat down for a moment?"

Sure, it was a little awkward, but I didn't mind. "My name is Brian Grazer. I have to admit I was watching you while I was on the phone. You just seemed to exude so much energy. But then I noticed that you're . . . paralyzed."

He didn't seem insulted, thank God. He just looked at me.

"I am," he said. "I have been for ten years."

"What is it like?" I said. Now, under a certain set of circumstances, that question might have seemed tactless or insensitive. But we'd shared a connection, a small moment of mutual recognition, and I didn't want to let the opportunity pass to know this man better.

I wasn't asking for novelty's sake. I asked because the risk of *not* understanding what his experiences were like seemed greater to me than the risk of asking and being rebuffed. To the best of my ability, I wanted to understand him. Is this tactless? Might the world not be a more humane place if we attempted to understand each other's circumstances a little more often? I think he saw the sincerity in my eyes.

He told me everything. That his name was Stephen and he worked in private equity. That his paralysis was the result of a progressive condition, a rare form of palsy. He told me about its various complications and how he'd learned to live with them. He had a lot of emotional range and appeared to be very accepting of his situation. I asked him how he spends his time, what he cares about, why he chose the career that he did. I sat with him and asked, and he answered. And he asked, and I answered. Somehow, it just flowed. Finally, I got up. I left our conversation having established a new friendship. We agreed we'd keep in touch, and so we have over the years.

Just last year in Paris, I was waiting in an Uber. It was my first time in the city since the terrorist attacks of November 2015 had taken place. In a series of coordinated attacks, 130 people were killed, many of them at the Bataclan, where the American rock band, Eagles of Death Metal, were playing. I had seen the coverage on the news and read about it in the paper. But I couldn't imagine what it was like for the individuals who called this city home.

Sitting in the backseat of the car, I looked down at my phone and thought about scrolling through my messages. Instead, I decided to engage my driver, Laurent, in conversation. I asked Laurent about the terrorist attack. How had it impacted him on a personal level? How did it affect his country? He put the car in park and turned around to look at me.

For the next forty minutes, Laurent and I talked, face to face, about the events that had happened and what it meant to be living in the current moment. It was an emotional conversation. I was surprised when Laurent confided that he was ashamed by the attacks. I had expected that he would be sad, frightened, angry—but ashamed? He explained how the terrorists had made the French feel a collective sense of powerlessness. I was moved by his revelation. It both deepened my understanding of the French people and opened a window into another way of seeing current events that I hadn't considered before.

When I was young, I only knew my small corner of California. Today, I have traveled all over the globe. But where I am is much less important than who I am with. Every time I connect with someone, I am transported somewhere new. And the best part is, it doesn't require a ticket or a suitcase or a GPS. All it takes is the curiosity and courage to initiate engagement with another human being, and the willingness to listen and learn with an open mind.

CHAPTER 15

In the Blink of an Eye

"You have power over your mind—not outside events.
Realize this, and you will find strength."

—Marcus Aurelius

Almost twenty years ago, I flew to Detroit, where we were shooting *8 Mile*. Admittedly one of my favorites among the movies I've produced, the film is the story of Eminem that emerged out of that fateful meeting in my office. After a few days on set—which was an ice-cold urban landscape in the dead of winter—I realized I needed to get out. I was craving sunshine and warmth. I decided to fly right to the set of another movie I was producing in Hawaii.

Blue Crush, a surf movie with a female cast, was set on the North Shore of Oahu. I had never been to this part of Hawaii before, so I was excited to check it out. I only knew what I had seen in other movies and on television: iconic surf breaks like Banzai Pipeline, Sunset Beach, and Waimea Bay. As we were touching down, I looked out the window to see the widest, most pristine beaches and the bluest ocean you could possibly imagine. If Detroit was a frigid nightmare, this looked like paradise. I was completely taken. After driving around for only an hour or two, I decided I wanted to live there—just like that. (This definitely marked one of the most extreme, "in the moment" decisions I've ever made in my life!) I found a house that felt good to me: a big, white Indonesian-style place with a blue-tile roof, right smack on Pipeline, the most legendary surf break in the Western Hemisphere.

My early days in Hawaii were everything I imagined they would be. I was beguiled by the North Shore's tropical beauty, the lush mountains I could see across Waimea Bay, and the laid-back vibe that pervaded the place. As usual, I had been feeling restless, my mind full of more stories than I could keep track of and too many things to think about, not least of which was the other movie I was making back in Detroit. I felt like I had found the perfect antidote, a world that seemed, on the surface at least, perfect—gorgeous, vibrant, and calm. I felt welcome.

We were using a local crew on *Blue Crush*—we'd hired only native Hawaiians, which is rare for productions there—in part because we wanted to integrate as seamlessly as we could within the community. So I was surprised when one day I came to the set and I noticed someone hanging around who didn't appear to belong there. He was physically imposing and had a hardened look about him. Although his interactions with the crew seemed friendly and familiar, in my eyes, this stranger was the definition of intimidating.

I soon discovered that this man—let's call him Jake—had

arrived with the express purpose of "helping us with some of our permitting and safety issues." He was actually a member of a group called the Da Hui, also known as the "Black Shorts" for the dark surf trunks they wore. The Da Hui organization formed on the North Shore in the mid-1970s with the intent of protecting the Pipeline against an incursion of mostly South African and Australian surfers. For Hawaiians, respect is an important concept, particularly when it comes to the ocean, their coveted natural resources, and their cultural heritage. As foreigners flocked to the area, crowding the waves, and big corporations started to commercialize a sport invented by their ancestors, some Hawaiians felt disrespected.

Groups like the Da Hui were determined to repel these outsiders and reclaim control of the ocean and sport that were so essential to who they were as a people. They would swim out into the water to disrupt competitions and demand that other surfers make way for them. They made it clear that they would do whatever they had to to preserve and protect what was theirs. Today, the Da Hui have traded their activist roots for more mainstream endeavors, like volunteering in the community, producing a clothing line, and overseeing water safety at surf contests. But their commitment to defending native Hawaiian culture is as strong as it ever was.

With Jake, the Da Hui had created a sort of extracurricular line item, a fee that wasn't part of the original budget for

Blue Crush. But after our production team conferred among ourselves, we decided that the easiest course of action was to pay up. This sort of strong-arming happens everywhere. It's the nature of shooting on location, so it didn't bother me too much.

Jake and I got along well, we even surfed together on occasion. Still, there was something about Jake's presence and demeanor that felt threatening to me. And it started to change the way I felt about the North Shore. Maybe my paradise wasn't so idyllic after all. Maybe it wasn't mine to begin with. As my preconceptions began to crack, my sense of security in this place turned to one of uncertainty.

While in Hawaii I was lucky enough to connect and form a friendship with Brock Little, who I mentioned had taught me to surf. Brock was a professional surfer and stuntman, a local who took me under his wing and showed me around. Among the many forces and factions on the North Shore, Brock was a kind of human Switzerland: strong but peace-loving, powerful but nonpartisan, on good terms with everybody. He was friendly with the Da Hui but not exactly a member. Through Brock, I came to know a lot about the regional culture, including proper etiquette out in the water.

When surfing with the locals, especially the more aggressive, alpha male–types, I learned that the one thing you should never do is look them in the eye when you're out on the water. If you mistakenly cut someone off on a wave *with-*

out looking them in the eye, it's one thing—an accident—but if you make eye contact beforehand, it is understood to be personal. Even if it was inadvertent, that look will be considered a show of disrespect and the locals will brand you with the "stink eye." If you're given the stink eye by a member of the Da Hui or another group, within an hour everybody on the North Shore will know and, from what I was led to understand, a broken car window or a trip to the hospital might follow. Whether those were idle threats or real dangers, I didn't know. But I didn't want to find out, either.

Sometimes not looking someone in the eye can be as meaningful as looking someone in the eye. Whom we look in the eye, when we look at them, how we look at them—all of these things shape our relationships within a given cultural context. In certain parts of the world, such as Nigeria or East Asia, for example, an excess of eye contact is considered disrespectful.[33] In Japan, school children are taught to look at the neck of the person they are speaking with to soften their gaze,[34] and in Iran, eye contact between men and women is strictly inappropriate.[35]

Even closer to home, there are surprising instances where direct eye contact is frowned upon. In the Minnesota Legislature, for example, Senate Rule 36.8 requires that "all remarks during debate should be addressed to the president." The Senate President resides at the front of the chamber, so even if a Senator is debating with someone behind them, they can't look at each other. They must face forward.[36] Apparently, this rule was established to promote civility by eliminating eye contact that might amplify aggression between representatives with opposing views.

In other situations, looking someone in the eye can lead you somewhere you don't want to go. When I produced the movie *The Chamber* (based on the John Grisham book) in 1996, we shot it at the Mississippi State Penitentiary—a death-row prison in the state, famously known as "Parchman Farm"—and the warden instructed us never to look the inmates in the eye when we passed. He knew that the inmates would *try* to make eye contact with us. For them, connection was an opportunity to get something they wanted but couldn't have. In other words, it was a tool for manipulation.

Out on the water with Jake, I minded my manners and he never branded me with the stink eye. But the experience of surfing with him revealed a new dimension of the culture to me and led me to think about eye contact in a new way. The eyes can help forge deep, trustful connections between people, but they are also brokers of power. With the Da Hui, you had to use your eyes carefully, to signal just the right amount of deference for the situation.

After we finished *Blue Crush* (which I'm proud to say became a cult phenomenon that helped bring surf culture—

specifically *female* surf culture—a little further into the mainstream), I spent a lot of time on the island. I went whenever I could break away and got to know it well. I wasn't exactly a local, but I wasn't what they call a *haole*, a non-native Hawaiian, either. I was accepted, or so I believed. Until one evening, when I was riding my bicycle along the trail to the same place I always went: past Sunset Beach to a place called V-Land.

V-Land was Da Hui territory, and I was humming along on my bike when two guys stepped out of the bushes and blocked my path.

"Oh, hey Brian." One of them moved toward me. He was pumped up like a bodybuilder, with tattoos covering his arms and knuckles. "What are you doing?"

I recognized him. I'd met him once or twice before. He was one of my surf buddy Jake's "associates," one of the most feared—and fearsome-looking—members of the Da Hui. He stepped closer to me. I knew immediately that this wasn't a social approach; these guys had something on their mind.

"I'm riding my bike," I said, keeping cool as best I could. The friend stepped forward now too.

"Brian, you haven't paid your taxes."

For a moment I wondered what he was talking about. *Taxes?* Then I realized he was trying to shake me down. Jake wringing us on the set of *Blue Crush* was one thing. But these guys wanted protection money from me personally.

"Oh, no," I said. "I've paid my taxes."

"We don't have any record of that," the tattooed guy said. "It's a new year, and we need new taxes."

I'm usually a pretty hyperactive guy: I thrive on the energy of other people and social situations, but in moments of physical danger—for whatever reason—I slow down. I've been held at gunpoint on two different occasions, and once was on an airplane when the electricity failed and it seemed likely we'd crash. This moment was a bit like those. My mind became very still.

"You know, we saw your girlfriend over at Foodland," the tattooed guy said. Foodland is a place where all the surfers congregate, the social hub of the North Shore. "She's very beautiful. I hope everything goes good for her. We'd hate for anything bad to happen to her."

Were they actually threatening her? Me? What exactly did they plan to do? This was serious. I had to have the right response. Rather than try to push back verbally or negotiate, I tried a different tack. Just as I had discovered that it wasn't a good idea to look any of the Da Hui in the eye on the water, so I had come to learn early on—also through my local friend Brock—to do the opposite while negotiating with them on land. Thank you, Brock.

Rather than look away, I did exactly what Brock had recommended. I looked at Tattoo Guy with a confident yet respectful gaze that was neither downcast nor too direct. I held his eyes for a long, silent moment.

"There's no problem here," I said finally. "I've paid my taxes. We're cool."

I shifted back onto my seat and pedaled away. To my amazement, they didn't try to stop me. I rode off toward the sunset. As soon as I did, my heart started pounding. What exactly had just happened?

Thinking about it now, I realize that I was able to defuse and stabilize the situation just by the way I used my eyes. In a single look, I was able to navigate a complicated power dynamic. On one hand, I was letting my antagonist know that I was not weak and that he could not scare me into submission. On the other, I was recognizing his strength and acknowledging a messy history in which I was linked to a long string of outsiders who had disrespected the Hawaiian people and their culture in all kinds of ways.

I may make my living as a producer, but what I really am is a storyteller. And stories are always about the communication of feelings. People have a tendency to see life as binary—right versus wrong, success versus failure—but feelings are more nuanced than that. They are both infinite in their variation and inarguable. You can't tell someone how they feel or how they experience the world. Feelings, like stories, are subjective, and what people need perhaps more than anything these days is to have their stories acknowledged and heard.

Don't we all want that? To be seen in a way that recognizes our own sense of who we are? I believe what happened that day with the two Da Hui was exactly that. I didn't attempt to challenge their story of themselves. Instead, I looked at them in a way that allowed me to maintain my personal agency, while acknowledging their strength, their authority, and their experience of the world.

CHAPTER 16

Honeymoon in the Holy Land

*"When God loves you, what can
be better than that?"*

—Aretha Franklin

I was raised both Jewish and Catholic: Jewish on my mother's side and Catholic on my father's. Until I was about ten, I basically lived the life of a Catholic. I was baptized as a baby (oddly, my Jewish mother had insisted that I be, probably to respect my father's beliefs), and I went to catechism every Sunday as a boy. I even remember visiting Santa Barbara during the Cuban Missile Crisis and running across the railroad tracks to pray for safety at a nearby mission.

Despite all this, the fear-based aspects of Catholicism—my childhood terror of being in sin, the fear of dying and going to hell—were a bit much for me. I was always more at home with the traditions of my Jewish heritage, which felt warmer and more alive to me. My grandma Sonia and I would go to temple a couple times a year and she would tell me stories about the Jewish faith. She had me over for seders and we celebrated the Jewish holidays together.

As I got older, my belief in God never waned, but I didn't particularly identify with either of the faith traditions in which I'd been raised.

Unlike me, Veronica was raised by a devout Catholic Filipina mother and a Catholic American father. She attended St. Columba Catholic elementary school and graduated from Georgetown, the oldest Catholic and Jesuit university in the country. She's deeply devoted to God and introduced me to her community at St. Monica Catholic Church. In fact, St. Monica is where we were married.

I often go to church with Veronica and have grown close with our pastor, Monsignor Lloyd Torgerson, a progressive, gifted, and beloved spiritual leader in the community and the city of Los Angeles. When he and I first met, what struck me immediately was the way he looked at me. I've met many priests in my life and have grown accustomed to seeing a hint of approval—or disapproval—in their eyes. Monsignor Torgerson's eyes, in contrast, hold nothing but deep love and humanity.

I had been brought up in a brand of Catholicism that emphasized guilt and judgment. The Catholicism that Monsignor preaches is completely different. A charismatic and gifted orator, Monsignor's weekly sermons are consistently powerful. No matter the theme, his message is always hopeful, relevant, and rooted in love. It hits you in the heart, not just the mind. Monsignor also has a special talent for using story and even his own personal fallacies and relatable struggles to help us make sense of our lives. Linking stories with inspiring reflection, he helps me reprioritize what matters most. I always walk away with something meaningful to reflect on, something that makes me think about the bigger picture of why we are here and what really matters in life. Monsignor and I have since become close friends, and he has had a profound impact on my spiritual journey.

When Veronica informed me one day that a group from our church would be traveling to Israel, I was interested but wary. I've never been one for group travel to begin with, and although I was feeling much more comfortable within Catholicism than I ever had before, I can't say I was 100 percent at ease with the idea of visiting Israel for the first time with a church group. That being said, I was definitely curious, and I knew the trip would mean a lot to Veronica. So I said yes and just like that the plan for our honeymoon was hatched.

Off we went on a nonstop flight from LA to Tel Aviv. We spent one night in Tel Aviv to regroup, and then set off again to join the group from St. Monica. Finally, we reached Tabgha, by the Sea of Galilee, where we would visit the Church of the Multiplication.

The Church of the Multiplication is the holiest of holy ground, where Christ performed the miracle of the loaves and fishes. The group was gathered around for Mass and, admittedly, I felt just a little out of place. As I often do, I found myself thinking of Grandma Sonia. But this time I wondered what she'd have made of my visit to the Holy Land with a

Catholic church group. I could feel a spiritual crisis setting in: Was I betraying her? Was I betraying God, and by extension, my own beliefs? What *did* I believe?

The idea of a spiritual crisis might sound a bit grand, but when you travel to a place like Israel, and when you feel connected to people you've loved both in the past (Grandma Sonia) and in the present (Veronica), you can't help but ponder the big questions.

We were about to take Communion when I noticed Eli standing in the background. Eli was our tour guide. Early on in our trip, I had struck up a personal conversation with him. I shared that I was Jewish by birth, raised as a confused Catholic, and that my wife was a practicing Catholic. Eli told me about what it was like to be an Israeli Jew living alongside Christians and Muslims in a land that each claims as its own. (Remarkably, at the center of Jerusalem, in an area about twice the size of the Mall in Washington, sit three major holy sites: the Al-Aqsa Mosque, the third holiest site in the world for Muslims; the Western Wall, part of the holiest site in the world for Jews; and the Church of the Holy Sepulchre, which marks the place where Christians believe Jesus was crucified, entombed, and resurrected.) Over the course of the trip, that one conversation between Eli and me turned into hours of discussion about our respective journeys into faith.

On this particular day, as Eli watched me with his gentle, inquisitive eyes, I could almost read his thoughts: *You have a Jewish mother and a Catholic father. Hmm . . . What's going through your mind, Brian?*

As I glanced back at him, the image of my grandmother came to me. Right then, I knew that I was not betraying her. I was not betraying God or myself. Rather, I was discovering who I was and what I believed. Despite the long and continuing history of religious conflicts there, I had a feeling of oneness with the people I saw. I felt deep love as I walked the city. I felt safe even though people don't think it's safe. Maybe I felt this because I was in a place of deep significance for all three religions. Maybe it was because of events from the Bible taking place in the very place I was walking. I'm not exactly sure what it was, but I felt it.

Two days later, our church group was planning to walk the Via Dolorosa, or the "Way of Suffering." This street in the Old City of Jerusalem is believed to be the very one that Jesus walked on the way to his crucifixion. Marked with the Stations of the Cross and terminating at the Church of the Holy Sepulcher, the Via Dolorosa is an important processional route for Christian pilgrims. As they travel the winding path, the pilgrims sing and take turns carrying the cross in imitation of Christ.

Not surprisingly, Veronica wanted to share this experience together. So we set our alarm for four in the morning and made our way in the pitch black from the King David

Hotel to the meeting point inside the walls of the Old City. We began. Our group of about forty people would take turns rotating who would carry the cross and who would follow and sing. At each of the fourteen stations, we recited a reading and prayer, then continued on to the next.

Monsignor tapped my shoulder. It was my turn. As I helped carry what must have been a ten- or twelve-foot, heavy wooden cross along the narrow, ancient walkway, the sun started to rise. We sang and made our way to the final stations within Golgotha, or Calvary, inside the church. As we walked in, I caught Eli's eye. This time, however, it was different. His gaze was not one of curiosity, but one of connection. We looked at each other for a long moment—two human beings sharing a spiritual quest.

CHAPTER 17

What It Means to Be Alive

*"I think that what we're seeking is an experience of being
alive, so that our life experiences on the purely physical
plane will have resonances with our own innermost being
and reality, so that we actually feel the rapture of being alive."*

—Joseph Campbell

Many years ago I was living in Malibu Colony, a residential
community near Pepperdine University. It was a temporary
situation while I was having construction done on my place
in the city. My house in Malibu was at the very end of the
colony, where the private access meets a public beach. Ordinarily, that beach was extremely crowded, so I liked to get up
early and have my coffee out on the deck, where I could enjoy
the view before it filled up. There were usually a few walkers
or surfers, but it was generally very calm. One morning I was
out—it was around seven thirty or so—and I found myself
utterly alone. The beach looked empty. I couldn't see a single
person from where I sat. As I sipped my coffee and stared
down the beach, however, I suddenly realized that there *was*
someone. Way, way down the beach and out closer to the
water, where the tide pools were, was a person lying on her

side. The sight was so strange. It took me a moment to realize I was looking at a human being. It took me another moment to realize that the person was in some sort of trouble. I couldn't detect any movement in her body.

I took off running, sprinting down the beach in her direction. It took me a good minute or two to get there. As I drew near, I saw two young girls standing over her on the beach. Their faces looked frightened. And right then, I realized that the person I'd raced out to help wasn't an adult but a teenager. Her body was pulsing and her arms were flailing. From the looks of it, she was having some sort of seizure.

I dropped down next to her. The tide was lapping right where she lay, and her face was in the water while her arms flapped at her sides. I rolled her onto her back and managed to drag her to dry sand. I don't have any formal medical training—I'm not an EMT or anything—but I remembered in high school there'd been a boy in my class who'd had an epileptic seizure in the cafeteria, so I knew to clear her mouth of obstruction. I pulled out a piece of gum.

She was barely conscious, clammy, and still. Her eyes, which to that point had been half-shut suddenly flashed open, revealing a blank stare without any trace of life or vitality. For a split second, my eyes fastened on hers and I felt certain she was going to die. Then, just as abruptly as they had popped open, her eyes closed again.

I desperately scanned the beach for another human being, someone who might summon help, and I felt an overwhelming sadness pulse through me. I felt powerless. I couldn't connect with her. I felt her slipping away. Whether or not you've ever seen someone dying, as I had only once before, the moment has a metaphysical quality, an overwhelming spiritual power.

The other time was when I was just nine years old. I'd had a paper route out in Northridge, California, where we lived, and while I was making my rounds one day I saw an elderly man lying in the middle of the street near an upside-down car. It was early in the morning and the accident had clearly taken place just moments before. A camper had smashed into his Chevy, causing it to flip over and fling him from the car. I could hear the ambulance siren, and people were starting to gather. Though I was only a young kid, I felt an incredible, palpable sadness then, too. This man was lifeless, gone. As I watched him lie there bleeding, I was stunned by what I now recognize as the pull of our shared humanity in that moment.

This moment on the beach was different. I was an adult and, by extension perhaps, a little closer to my own mortality, but this girl was just a kid.

"Georgia!" a woman's voice yelled.

It all took place within a span of seconds. It felt much longer, but it was almost instantaneous. I looked over my shoulder and—thank God!—there was a woman sprinting toward us.

"Georgia!"

I realized as she approached that I knew her: the woman was Melissa Mathison, the late screenwriter of *E.T.*, who was at that time married to Harrison Ford. She happened to be the girl's mother. I think—it's hard to recall—I yelled to *her* to get help and dial 911.

Fortunately, there's a station right outside the colony gate, and the paramedics arrived almost immediately. But until they did, I stayed right where I was, kneeling down beside the girl and searching her semiconscious face. I was deep inside that fragile moment; I had no control over what would happen next. And that fundamental *uncertainty* seemed to me to exemplify the crux of the human experience. Would she live? Who knew. The part of the experience that remains indelible is the connection I felt, not just to her as a person, but to her fate.

She was airlifted to UCLA Medical Center via helicopter. Thankfully, she fully recovered.

A few years later, about five years after the incident, I was walking through the lobby of the Mercer Hotel where I always stay when I'm in New York. I noticed Harrison Ford sitting on one of the couches. At the time of the incident, I only knew him as an actor. I'd been trying to make a movie about the Worcester Cold Storage and Warehouse Co. fire, a brutal and terrifying blaze that killed six firefighters in Massachusetts in 1999, and Harrison had agreed to star in it, but the film never got off the ground. He's a very strong guy, slightly brusque but powerful, as you'd probably expect from the roles he plays. He has tremendous integrity. Right after he found out what had happened, he called to thank me. For a long time I never told anyone what had happened, aside from my family. It seemed like another reality.

As I was crossing the Mercer lobby, Harrison called out to me. He waved me over to where he was sitting with a young woman in her early twenties.

"Come have a drink with us."

I joined them. The bar was crowded, as it happened to be Fashion Week, and so the three of us found ourselves huddled together in this densely packed room.

"Do you recognize this girl?" he said. "This is my daughter, Georgia."

Of course I recognized her, and she recognized me too. I was relieved to see her alert and full of life. We sat together and had a glass of wine. It felt like we were bound together by an indescribable connection—the ineffable experience of our shared humanity and fleeting mortality.

We are all human beings. We all have emotions. We all have something to share. We are made for connection. It is the source of growth, discovery, joy, and meaning in our short, sweet time here on Earth. We need only be willing to open our minds and our hearts and choose to *see* the people standing with us face to face. Whether the connection lasts a moment or a lifetime, whether it's easy or challenging, we are always better for it.

Acknowledgments

Sage, Riley, Patrick, and Thomas: I hope you'll take in these stories and lessons from my life as you develop your own ways of creating meaningful connections and finding fulfillment within yourselves and out in the world. May our birthday speeches always live on.

This book has evolved thanks to the wise and creative input from friends and colleagues, among them Malcolm Gladwell, Bryan Lourd, Adam Grant, Michael Rosenberg, Risa Gertner, Julie Oh, Tara Polacek, Simon Sinek, Will Rosenfeld, Stephanie Frerich, and everybody else who offered guidance along the way. I want to especially thank our friends Jenna Abdou and Samantha Vinograd for the heartfelt heavy lifting, especially when the countdown was on. You understood the vision and made it better. Thank you, Jenn Hallam: you are every bit the superstar that Simon described at Toscana.

Almost every weekend, I see a close friend of mine, face

to face, for coffee. Thank you, Bob Iger, for the immeasurable friendship.

Jon Karp, the president and publisher of Simon and Schuster, loved the idea of eye contact and personal connection from the very start. Thank you for your patience and encouragement.

I am deeply grateful to my friend, the celebrated artist Mark Bradford, who generously created the "FACE TO FACE" artwork for this book. I have always been deeply moved by his story. Surviving by working in his mother's beauty shop in Crenshaw, he didn't have the money or opportunity to become an artist until his forties. It's super difficult and rare to reach his level of achievement as an artist when starting at that age. He is, and always will be, an original voice in our world.

Thank you to novelist and screenwriter Matthew Specktor, who helped form the book when it was just a whisper of an idea. We met over many breakfasts of huevos rancheros on the back porch while he took in my stories.

In my business as a movie and television producer, I make qualitative decisions every day. Whenever I make one of those decisions and tell myself it's "good enough," it nearly always means it's sh*tty. With this book, there was a point when the manuscript had been delivered, the book was listed on Amazon, and I thought we were ready to go. The day of the deadline, my brilliantly candid wife, Veronica, pulled me aside and said the book was only "good enough."

I understood immediately. She was the catalyst—as well as my thought partner—who spurred me to dive back in and take the extra time to make this book better. She was relentless in pushing me hard, and I am forever grateful.

Every day, Veronica teaches me and our children about genuine human connection, not through words but in the way she takes the time to see people, listen to them, and make them feel like they matter. She is my blessing, and my true collaborator on this book, and in life. I'm grateful to God for you.

Notes

1. "Can Relationships Boost Longevity and Well-Being?" *Harvard Health Publishing*, Harvard Medical School, June 2017, https://www.health.harvard.edu/mental-health/can-relationships-boost-longevity-and-well-being/.
2. "An Epidemic of Loneliness," *The Week*, January 6, 2019, https://theweek.com/articles/815518/epidemic-loneliness/.
3. Ceylan Yeginsu, "U.K. Appoints a Minister for Loneliness," *New York Times*, January 17, 2018, https://www.nytimes.com/2018/01/17/world/europe/uk-britain-loneliness.html.
4. Maria Russo, "The Eyes Have It," *New York Times*, March 25, 2015, https://www.nytimes.com/interactive/2015/03/25/books/review/25childrens.html.
5. Flora Carr, "Rapping for Freedom," *Time*, May 17, 2018, https://time.com/collection-post/5277970/sonita-alizadeh-next-generation-leaders.
6. Steven Kotler, "Social Flow: 9 Social Triggers for Entering Flow," Medium, Feb 21, 2014, https://medium.com/@kotlersteven/social-flow-b04436fac167.
7. "Steven Kotler on Lyme Disease and the Flow State," Joe Rogan Experience Podcast #873, YouTube, November 21, 2016, https://www.youtube.com/watch?v=X_yq-4remO0.
8. Jill Suttie, "Why Curious People Have Better Relationships," *Greater Good*, May 31, 2017, https://greatergood.berkeley.edu/article/item/why_curious_people_have_better_relationships/.

9. "Winfrey's Commencement Address," *The Harvard Gazette*, May 31, 2013, https://news.harvard.edu/gazette/story/2013/05/winfreys-commencement-address/.

10. Sue Shellenbarger, "Just Look Me in the Eye Already," *The Wall Street Journal*, May 28, 2013, https://www.wsj.com/articles/SB10001424127887324809804578511290822228174/.

11. Jill O'Rourke, "For Riz Ahmed, There's a Difference Between 'Diversity' And 'Representation' In Media," *A Plus*, October 10, 2018, https://articles.aplus.com/film-forward/riz-ahmed-trevor-noah-diversity-representation/.

12. Simon Sinek, "How Great Leaders Inspire Action," TEDx Puget Sound, September 2009, https://www.ted.com/talks/simon_sinek_how_great_leaders_inspire_action?language=en/.

13. "The City: U.S. Jury Convicts Heroin Informant," *New York Times*, August 25, 1984.

14. Mark Jacobson, "The Return of Superfly," *New York Magazine*, August 14, 2000, http://nymag.com/nymetro/news/people/features/3649/.

15. Ayanna Prescod, "9 Fashion Staples You Need Inspired by Cookie Lyon from 'Empire,'" *Vibe*, January 14, 2015, https://www.vibe.com/2015/01/9-fashion-staples-you-need-inspired-by-cookie-lyon-from-empire/.

16. Adam Gopnik, "Can Science Explain Why We Tell Stories?," *The New Yorker*, May 18, 2012, https://www.newyorker.com/books/page-turner/can-science-explain-why-we-tell-stories/.

17. Mike Fleming Jr, "Netflix Wins 'Tunga,' Animated Musical from Zimbabwe-Born Newcomer Godwin Jabangwe; First Deal out of Talent Hatchery Imagine Impact 1," *Deadline*, February 14, 2019, https://deadline.com/2019/02/tunga-netflix-animated-musical-zimbabwe-newcomer-godwin-ja-bangwe-imagine-impact-1-1202557570/.

18. Stephen Covey, *7 Habits of Highly Effective People* (New York: Simon & Schuster, 1989), 251.

19. Celeste Heiter, "Film Review: The Man Who Would Be King,"
    ThingsAsian, September 29, 2006, http://thingsasian.com/story/
    film-review-man-who-would-be-king/.

20. Martin Stezano, "One Man Exposed the Secrets of the Freemasons.
    His Disappearance Led to Their Downfall," January 24, 2019,
    https://www.history.com/news/freemason-secrets-revealed/.

21. Mo Rocca, "Inside the Secret World of the Freemasons," *CBS News*,
    December 8, 2013, https://www.cbsnews.com/news/inside-the
    -secret-world-of-the-freemasons/.

22. Stezano, "One Man Exposed the Secrets of the Freemasons. His
    Disappearance Led to Their Downfall."

23. "List of Presidents of the United States Who Were Freemasons,"
    Wikipedia, accessed April 14, 2019, https://en.wikipedia.org/wiki/
    List_of_Presidents_of_the_United_States_who_were_Freemasons.

24. Rocca, "Inside the Secret World of the Freemasons."

25. "Freemasonry Under the Nazi Regime," *Holocaust Encyclopedia*,
    United States Holocaust Memorial Museum, accessed April 14,
    2019, https://www.ushmm.org/wlc/en/article.php?ModuleId=
    10007187/.

26. "Suppression of Freemasonry," *Wikipedia*, accessed April 14, 2019,
    https://en.wikipedia.org/wiki/Suppression_of_Freemasonry.

27. "A Standard of Masonic Conduct," *Short Talk Bulletin*, 7, no.12
    (December 1929), http://www.masonicworld.com/education/files/
    artfeb02/standard%20of%20masonic%20conduct.htm.

28. Adrian Ward, Kristen Duke, Ayelet Gneezy, and Maarten Bos,
    "Brain Drain: The Mere Presence of One's Own Smartphone
    Reduces Available Cognitive Capacity," *Journal of the Association
    for Consumer Research* 2, no. 2 (April 2017), https://www.journals.
    uchicago.edu/doi/10.1086/691462.

29. Olivia Yasukawa, "Senegal's 'Dead Sea': Salt Harvesting in the
    Strawberry-Pink Lake," *CNN*, June 27, 2014, https://www.cnn.com
    /2014/06/27/world/africa/senegals-dead-sea-lake-retba/index
    .html.

30. Kevin E. G. Perry, "Where the Magic Happens: Baaba Maal Interviewed," *The Quietus*, January 19, 2016, https://thequietus.com /articles/19559-baaba-maal-interview/.

31. Brian Grazer, *A Curious Mind* (New York: Simon & Schuster, 2015).

32. Rahima Nasa, "Timeline: How the Crisis in Venezuela Unfolded," *PBS Frontline*, February 22, 2019, https://www.pbs.org/wgbh/ frontline/article/timeline-how-the-crisis-in-venezuela-unfolded/.

33. Geri-Ann Galanti, *Caring for Patients from Different Cultures* (Philadelphia: University of Pennsylvania Press, 2004), 34, https:// books.google.com/books?id=nVgeOxUL3cYC&pg=PA34#v= onepage&q&f=false/.

34. Robert T. Moran, Philip R. Harris, Sarah V. Moran, *Managing Cultural Differences: Global Leadership Strategies for the 21st Century* (Butterworth-Heinemann, 2007), retrieved December 17, 2010, 64.

35. Alicia Raeburn, "10 Places Where Eye-Contact Is Not Recommended (10 Places Where the Locals Are Friendly)," *The Travel*, September 12, 2018, https://www.thetravel.com /10-places-where-eye-contact-is-not-recommended-10-places -where-the-locals-are-friendly/.

36. Ailsa Chang, "What Eye Contact—and Dogs—Can Teach Us About Civility in Politics," NPR, May 8, 2015, https://www.npr.org/sections /itsallpolitics/2015/05/08/404991505/what-eye-contact-and-dogs -can-teach-us-about-civility-in-politics/.